Dream Skiathos: A Tr Guide

Daniel Hunter

All rights reserved. No part of this publication may be reproduced, distributed, or transmitted in any form or by any means, including photocopying, recording, or other electronic or mechanical methods, without the prior written permission of the publisher, except in the case of brief quotations embodied in critical reviews and certain other noncommercial uses permitted by copyright law.

Copyright © (Daniel Hunter) (2024).

TABLE OF CONTENTS

Chapter 1. Introduction..................... 10
    1.1. Welcome to Skiathos... 10
    1.2. Why Visit Skiathos?... 11

Chapter 2. Planning Your Trip......................... 15
    2.1. Best Time to Visit.. 15
    2.2. How to Get There..16
    2.3. Travel Essentials.. 19
    2.4. Currency and Budgeting................................... 21
    2.5. Health and Safety Tips...................................... 24
    2.6. Language and Useful Phrases.......................... 27

Chapter 3. Accommodations........................... 31
    3.1. Types of Accommodations................................ 31
    3.2. Top Hotels for Couples......................................34
    3.3. Family-Friendly Resorts....................................37
    3.4. Budget Stays for Solo Travelers....................... 39

Chapter 4. Getting Around...........................43
    4.1. Public Transportation.......................................43
    4.2. Car Rentals.. 46
    4.3. Biking and Walking...48

Chapter 5. Exploring Skiathos....................... 53
    5.1. Main Attractions.. 53
    5.2. Hidden Gems..56
    5.3. Beaches...58
    5.4. Historical Sites and Museums.......................... 61
    5.5. Natural Wonders and Hiking Trails................ 64

Chapter 6. Activities and Adventures............... 67
    6.1. Water Sports.. 67

6.2. Boat Tours and Island Hopping........................69
6.3. Hiking and Nature Walks................................72
6.4. Cultural Activities and Workshops................... 74
6.5. Nightlife and Entertainment............................ 77
Chapter 7. Dining and Cuisine........................81
7.1. Traditional Greek Cuisine............................... 81
7.2. Best Restaurants for Couples........................... 83
7.3. Family-Friendly Dining....................................86
7.4. Budget-Friendly Eats...................................... 89
7.5. Local Markets and Street Food........................ 92
Chapter 8. Shopping...95
8.1. Local Markets and Souvenirs........................... 95
8.2. Boutiques and Artisan Shops...........................98
8.3. Shopping Tips and Etiquette......................... 100
Chapter 9. Itineraries....................................... 105
9.1. Weekend Getaway...105
9.2. 5-Day Itinerary.. 108
    Day 1: Arrival and Beach Bliss......................... 108
    Day 2: Island Hopping and Beach Exploration..... 108
    Day 3: Cultural Exploration and Relaxation....109
    Day 4: Adventure and Beach Hopping............ 109
    Day 5: Farewell to Skiathos............................. 110
9.3. 7-Day Itinerary..110
    Day 1: Arrival and Relaxation........................... 110
    Day 2: Beach Hopping and Water Sports......... 111
    Day 3: Island Exploration and History............. 111
    Day 4: Sailing and Island Hopping...................112
    Day 5: Relaxation and Indulgence....................112

- Day 6: Adventure and Nature............................ 113
- Day 7: Farewell to Skiathos................................113
- 9.4. Itinerary for Solo Travelers.............................114
  - Days 1-2: Relax and Explore Skiathos Town.... 114
  - Days 3-4: Island Hopping and Beach Bliss...... 114
  - Days 5-6: Adventure and Relaxation................ 115
  - Day 7: Farewell to Skiathos................................115
- 9.5. Itinerary for Families.. 116
  - Day 1: Arrival and Beach Bliss......................... 116
  - Day 2: Exploring the Island and Waterpark Fun.. 117
  - Day 3: Pirate Adventure and Relaxation.......... 117
  - Day 4: Beach Hopping and Farewell................ 118
- 9.6. Romantic Getaway for Couples........................ 119
  - Day 1: Arrival and Relaxation........................... 119
  - Day 2: Beach Bliss and Island Exploration......120
  - Day 3: Monastery and Sunset Cruise............... 120
  - Day 4: Island Hopping and Beach Escape........121
  - Day 5: Farewell to Paradise.............................. 121

Chapter 10. Traveling with Kids..................... 123
- 10.1. Kid-Friendly Attractions................................ 123
  - Beach Bliss for the Whole Family....................123
  - Adventures for Young Explorers...................... 124
  - Dining with the Little Ones............................. 124
- 10.2. Activities for Children....................................125
  - Beach Bliss.. 125
  - Island Adventures...126
  - Other Fun Activities... 126
- 10.3. Tips for Parents.. 127

Choosing the Right Accommodation.................127
Beach Bliss for the Whole Family....................128
Family-Friendly Activities...............................128
Dining with Kids...129
Tips for Traveling with Kids............................129
10.4. Family Accommodation Recommendations.130
Hotels and Resorts..130
Apartments and Villas......................................130
Tips for Choosing Family Accommodation:.....131

Chapter 11. Traveling Solo.............................133
11.1. Safety Tips for Solo Travelers.........................133
General Safety Tips..133
Personal Safety..133
Health and Safety..134
Making Connections...134
11.2. Best Places to Meet People..............................135
Beach Bars and Clubs..135
Taverns and Restaurants...................................136
Bars and Clubs...136
Boat Trips and Excursions................................136
Water Sports and Activities..............................137
Tips for Meeting People....................................137
11.3. Solo Activities and Experiences......................138
Beach Bliss and Solitude...................................138
Exploring the Island Alone...............................139
Relax and Recharge...139
Connecting with Other Travelers.....................140
11.4. Budget-Friendly Tips.......................................141
Accommodation..141

6

    Transportation... 141
    Food and Drink..142
    Activities... 142
    Additional Tips.. 143
Chapter 12. Romantic Getaways...................... 145
  12.1. Romantic Activities and Spots...................... 145
    Romantic Activities...145
    Romantic Spots..146
  12.2. Couple's Itinerary..147
    Day 1: Arrival and Relaxation........................147
    Day 2: Beach Hopping and Adventure............ 147
    Day 3: Island Exploration and Pampering...... 148
    Day 4: Sailing and Sunset Cruise..................... 148
    Day 5: Farewell to Paradise.............................. 149
  12.3. Best Restaurants for Couples.........................150
    Fine Dining with a View................................. 150
    Intimate and Charming...................................151
    Seaside Serenity.. 151
  12.4. Honeymoon Ideas.. 152
    Romantic Retreats:..152
    Intimate Experiences:......................................153
    Adventurous Spirits:..153
    Culinary Delights:..154
    Unforgettable Moments:................................. 154
Chapter 13. Day Trips and Excursions............ 157
  13.1. Nearby Islands... 157
    Skopelos: The Green Island............................157
    Alonissos: Marine Paradise............................. 157
    Skyros: Authentic Greece................................ 158

13.2. Cultural and Historical Day Trips...................159
    Island Hopping for History and Charm........... 159
    Mainland Adventures: Delve into Greece's Past.... 160
    Sailing and Exploring: Discover Hidden Gems..... 160

13.3. Nature and Adventure Day Trips................... 161
    Island Hopping Adventures.............................161
    Exploring the Island's Interior......................... 162
    Water-Based Adventures.................................162
    Day Trips with a Purpose............................... 163

Chapter 14. Events and Festivals..................... 165

14.1. Annual Festivals... 165
    Religious Celebrations.....................................165
    Commemorative Events................................. 165
    Cultural Celebrations......................................166

14.2. Local Events Calendar................................167
    Summertime Celebrations..............................167
    Religious Festivities.......................................168
    Other Notable Events.................................... 168

14.3. Celebrations and Traditions......................... 169
    Religious Celebrations....................................169
    Local Festivals and Events............................. 170
    Traditions and Customs.................................. 171

Chapter 15. Practical Information................... 173

15.1. Emergency Contacts.. 173
    General Emergency Numbers:......................... 173
    Local Emergency Contacts:............................. 173
    Additional Useful Numbers:............................173

Medical Emergencies:..................................174
15.2. Local Laws and Customs...............................174
    Laws and Regulations:....................................174
    Local Customs and Etiquette:..........................175
15.3. Internet and Connectivity............................. 176
    Mobile Data and Wi-Fi.................................... 176
    Internet Cafes...177

Chapter 16. Useful Resources......................... 179
16.1. Travel Apps and Websites............................. 179
    Essential Travel Apps:...................................... 179
    Helpful Websites:... 179
    Additional Tips:...180
16.2. Contact Information for Tourist Services...... 181
    Local Tourist Information:............................... 181
    Other Helpful Resources:................................. 181

Chapter 17. Conclusion..................................... 183
17.1. Final Tips and Advice..................................... 183

The Nymph of Skiathos..................................... 185

Chapter 1. Introduction

1.1. Welcome to Skiathos

Welcome to Skiathos, a gem in the Aegean Sea renowned for its stunning natural beauty, vibrant culture, and warm hospitality. As you embark on your journey through this enchanting island, prepare to be captivated by its golden beaches, crystal-clear waters, and lush pine forests. Skiathos is not just a destination; it's an experience filled with rich history, delicious cuisine, and a lively nightlife that will leave you with unforgettable memories. Whether you're an adventurer seeking thrilling water sports, a history buff exploring ancient ruins, or someone simply looking to unwind on serene shores, Skiathos has something special for everyone. Dive in and let this travel guide be your companion as you discover the magic of Skiathos. Welcome to your dream getaway!

1.2. Why Visit Skiathos?

Skiathos, the jewel of the Sporades archipelago, offers an unparalleled blend of natural splendor, cultural richness, and modern comforts. Here are some compelling reasons to visit this enchanting island:

Stunning Beaches

Skiathos boasts over 60 pristine beaches, each with its own unique charm. From the famous Koukounaries Beach, known for its golden sands and lush pine forest, to the secluded Lalaria Beach, accessible only by boat and renowned for its striking white pebbles and azure waters, Skiathos is a beach lover's paradise.

Crystal Clear Waters
The island's waters are some of the clearest in the Aegean, making it a perfect destination for swimming, snorkeling, and diving. The vibrant marine life and underwater landscapes offer an unforgettable experience for water enthusiasts.

Rich History and Culture
Skiathos has a storied past, reflected in its historic sites and cultural landmarks. Explore the medieval Castle of Skiathos, the Monastery of Evangelistria, where the first Greek flag was created, and the charming old town with its narrow streets and traditional architecture.

Outdoor Adventures
For those who love the outdoors, Skiathos offers numerous hiking trails through verdant landscapes, dense forests, and scenic viewpoints. The island's terrain is ideal for trekking, with trails leading to hidden coves, ancient ruins, and panoramic vistas.

Lively Nightlife
Skiathos is famous for its vibrant nightlife. The island offers a variety of bars, clubs, and tavernas that come alive after sunset. Whether you prefer a

quiet drink by the sea or dancing the night away, Skiathos caters to all tastes.

Delicious Cuisine
Greek cuisine is a highlight of any visit to Skiathos. Enjoy fresh seafood, traditional dishes, and local specialties at the island's numerous tavernas and restaurants. Don't miss trying the island's fresh fish, mezes, and the famous Skiathos honey.

Welcoming Hospitality
The people of Skiathos are known for their warm hospitality and friendly nature. Visitors often leave with a sense of having made new friends and experienced genuine Greek hospitality.

Easy Accessibility
Skiathos is easily accessible by air and sea, with regular flights and ferry services connecting it to Athens and other parts of Greece. Its well-developed infrastructure makes it a convenient and comfortable destination for travelers.

Cinematic Beauty
Fans of the film "Mamma Mia!" will recognize Skiathos as one of the main filming locations. The island's picturesque landscapes and charming spots

featured in the movie add a touch of Hollywood magic to your visit.

Whether you're seeking relaxation, adventure, culture, or a bit of everything, Skiathos promises a fulfilling and memorable holiday experience. With its breathtaking scenery, rich traditions, and modern amenities, Skiathos is a destination that truly has it all.

Chapter 2. Planning Your Trip

2.1. Best Time to Visit

Skiathos basks in a glorious Mediterranean climate, tempting visitors with long, sunny days and warm seas. But to really capture the perfect Greek island experience, timing is key. Here's a rundown of what Skiathos offers across the seasons to help you decide when to book your escape:

Sun-soaked days and lively nights (June-August): This is peak season in Skiathos. Expect scorching temperatures, crystal-clear waters ideal for swimming, and a vibrant atmosphere. The island comes alive with beach bars, bustling restaurants, and energetic nightlife. However, this peak popularity comes with a price tag – accommodation and flights will be at their most expensive, and popular beaches can get crowded.

Shoulder seasons for serenity (May-June & September-October): If you crave a touch more peace without sacrificing sunshine, consider the shoulder seasons. May and June offer pleasant temperatures, blooming wildflowers, and a chance to snag a good deal on accommodation. September is another gem, with the summer crowds thinning but the weather still warm and sunny. You'll also find calmer seas, perfect for watersports enthusiasts.

Island charm off the beaten path (April & October-November): For a truly tranquil escape, consider the very beginning or end of the season. April offers spring's awakening with blooming flowers and fresh air. October and November bring even lower prices and a chance to experience the island's quieter side, with many tavernas and shops still open. Be aware though, some facilities may be closed during this time.

Skiathos beyond the beach (December-March): While the island sleeps off-season, Skiathos retains a certain charm.Temperatures are mild, and you'll practically have the island to yourself. This is a great time for exploring the charming villages and historical sites at your own pace. However, many restaurants and shops close during this time, so be sure to research what's open beforehand.

2.2. How to Get There

Here's how to navigate your journey to this captivating island:

Ferry: The most popular and scenic option for reaching Skiathos is by ferry. Ferries depart from several mainland Greece ports, offering year-round and seasonal connections. Here's a breakdown of the main routes:

- **Volos:** This is the champion of speed and frequency for ferry travel to Skiathos. High-speed ferries whisk you away to the island in a mere 1 hour, while conventional ferries take approximately 2.5 hours. The best part? Ferries depart daily throughout the year, ensuring flexibility in your travel plans.
- **Mantoudi:** Situated on the island of Evia, Mantoudi provides another year-round ferry route to Skiathos. The journey takes between 1.5 and 4.5 hours, depending on the ferry type. So, whether you prefer a quick crossing or want to savor the sea views, there's a ferry option for you on this route.
- **Seasonal Routes:** During the peak summer season, additional ferry routes come alive, offering connections from Agios Konstantinos in Phthiotis and Thessaloniki in Northern Greece. These routes cater to the surge in tourism and provide more options for travelers coming from different parts of Greece.

Important Note: Keep in mind that there are no direct ferries to Skiathos from Athens. If you're flying into Athens International Airport (ATH), you'll need to take a bus to one of the port cities mentioned above before hopping on a ferry.Luckily, buses connect Athens to these port towns frequently, making the journey smooth.

Flights: For those seeking a quicker connection, Skiathos boasts a small airport (JSI) with seasonal connections from various European cities. This can be a great option if you're short on time or if flights align better with your travel plans.However, flights tend to be less frequent compared to ferries, so be sure to check schedules and book well in advance,especially during peak season.

Next Steps: Once you've chosen your preferred route, ferry companies and online booking platforms offer convenient options for booking your tickets. Consider factors like travel time, cost, and amenities offered by different ferry operators to make an informed decision.

Additionally, if you're traveling with a car or motorbike, some ferries allow vehicle transport. Be sure to check with the ferry company in advance and book this service if needed, as space can be limited.

2.3. Travel Essentials

To make the most of your island escape, here's a rundown of travel essentials to ensure you pack perfectly for your Skiathos adventure:

Beach Essentials:

- Swimwear (pack a couple of options, considering quick drying materials for island hopping)
- Beach towel (lightweight and quick-drying is ideal)
- Hat with a brim for sun protection
- Sunglasses (polarized lenses help reduce glare)
- Reef-safe sunscreen (protect yourself and the beautiful marine life)
- Cover-up for walks to and from the beach
- Beach bag for essentials like sunscreen, water bottle, and snacks

Island Exploration:

- Comfortable walking shoes for exploring charming villages and historical sites

- Light, breathable clothing for hot summer days (think sundresses, shorts, and breezy shirts)
- A long-sleeved shirt or light sweater for cooler evenings
- Pants or a long skirt for visiting monasteries or religious sites (respectful attire is appreciated)

Don't Forget:

- Comfortable sandals or wedges for evenings out
- Personal toiletries and medications
- A reusable water bottle to stay hydrated (tap water is safe to drink in Greece, but bottled water is readily available)
- Camera to capture those unforgettable moments
- Power bank to keep your devices charged
- Adaptor if you're traveling from a country with different electrical outlets
- European Health Insurance Card (EHIC) or travel insurance for peace of mind

Optional Extras:

- A good book for lazy afternoons under the olive trees

- Waterproof phone case for beachside snaps
- Cash for smaller purchases and local vendors (ATMs are widely available, but having some cash is always handy)
- Phrasebook or Greek language app to learn a few basic phrases (a little effort goes a long way with the locals!)

Remember:

- Check the weather forecast before you pack, but expect mostly sunny days with warm temperatures.
- Pack light, loose-fitting clothing that allows for layering due to occasional breezes.
- Opt for natural fabrics like cotton and linen to stay cool in the summer heat.
- Most importantly, pack your sense of adventure and get ready to experience the magic of Skiathos!

2.4. Currency and Budgeting

Skiathos, like all of Greece, uses the **Euro (€)** as its official currency. Saying goodbye to drachmas happened back in 2002, so you won't need to exchange any forgotten currency.

Budgeting for Paradise:

Skiathos can be a budget-friendly paradise or a luxurious escape, depending on your spending style. Here's a breakdown to help you estimate your costs:

Accommodation: Prices vary depending on the season, location, and type of accommodation. Budget-friendly options include hostels, guesthouses, and studios. Mid-range hotels and apartments offer more amenities, while luxury villas and beachfront resorts cater to those seeking a splurge.

Food: Delicious Greek meals can be surprisingly affordable. Gyros, souvlaki, and fresh salads are budget-friendly options. Tavernas by the beach tend to be pricier. Consider self-catering in your accommodation to save on meals. Stock up on groceries and local specialties at the island's supermarkets and bakeries.

Activities: Many beaches are free to access, while some require renting sun loungers and umbrellas. Boat trips, water sports, and historical site visits typically have entrance fees. Consider purchasing a multi-activity pass if you plan on doing a lot of excursions.

Transportation: Getting around Skiathos is easy. The main town offers local buses that connect to popular beaches and villages. Taxis are readily available, but be sure to agree on a fare before getting in. Renting a car or scooter gives you more freedom to explore, but factor in gas prices and potential parking fees.

General Tips:

- **Cash vs. Card:** While credit cards are accepted at most restaurants, shops, and hotels, it's always a good idea to carry some cash for smaller purchases, taxis, and local vendors. ATMs are widely available, but carrying some Euros from your home country avoids potential foreign transaction fees.
- **Daily Budget:** A good starting point for budgeting is €50-€100 per person per day for food and activities. This can be adjusted based on your spending habits. Accommodation costs will vary the most, so factor that in when creating your overall budget.
- **Free Activities:** Take advantage of free activities like swimming at the beach, exploring charming villages, and hiking scenic trails. Pack a picnic lunch and enjoy

the beautiful outdoors without spending a dime.

Remember:

- Planning and researching prices in advance helps you create a realistic budget.
- Look for deals and discounts, especially during the shoulder seasons (spring and fall).
- Embrace the local way of life and avoid tourist traps that might inflate your costs.
- Most importantly, focus on creating unforgettable memories, not breaking the bank!

2.5. Health and Safety Tips

While Skiathos promises carefree days basking in the Aegean sunshine, a little preparation can go a long way in ensuring a healthy and safe vacation. Here are some health and safety tips to keep in mind for your trip:

Sun Safety:

- The Mediterranean sun is strong, so pack high-factor (SPF 30 or higher),

broad-spectrum sunscreen and reapply frequently, especially after swimming or toweling off.
- Seek shade during the hottest part of the day (typically between 12 pm and 4 pm).
- Wear a hat with a brim and sunglasses for additional protection.
- Stay hydrated by drinking plenty of water throughout the day.

Safety in the Sun and Sea:

- Be aware of water conditions and heed any posted warnings about strong currents or rip tides.
- Swim at beaches with lifeguards on duty, especially if you're traveling with children.
- When exploring rocky coastlines, wear sturdy shoes to avoid slips and falls.
- If you're planning on water sports, ensure proper equipment and follow safety instructions.

General Health:

- Pack any medications you require and bring a copy of your prescriptions in case you need refills.

- Mosquitoes can be present, so consider insect repellent, particularly in the evenings.
- Be mindful of what you eat, especially in the heat. Opt for fresh, cooked meals and avoid leaving food out for extended periods.
- If you have any allergies, inform your accommodation and restaurants beforehand.
- Basic medical care is available on the island, but consider travel insurance for comprehensive coverage.

Staying Safe:

- Petty theft can occur anywhere, so keep valuables secure in your hotel safe or a money belt.
- Be mindful of your belongings on the beach, especially when swimming.
- Let someone know if you're planning on venturing off the beaten path for hikes or explorations.
- Familiarize yourself with emergency numbers for police, ambulance, and fire services.

Additional Tips:

- Pack a small first-aid kit with basic supplies like bandages, antiseptic wipes, and pain relievers.
- Carry a photocopy of your passport and important documents in case the originals are lost or stolen.
- Download offline maps or roaming data packages for your phone to stay connected
- Learn a few basic Greek phrases - it's a kind gesture that the locals appreciate.

By following these tips, you can ensure a healthy and enjoyable vacation in Skiathos. Remember, a little planning goes a long way in allowing you to relax, unwind, and fully embrace the island's magic!

2.6. Language and Useful Phrases

While English is spoken in many tourist areas of Skiathos, immersing yourself a little in the local language can enhance your experience. Greek is a beautiful language, and even a few basic phrases will go a long way with the friendly Skiathos locals. Here's a helpful guide to get you started:

Greetings and Essentials:

- Γεια σας (Yá sas) - Hello (formal)
- Γεια σου (Yá sou) - Hello (informal)
- Καλημέρα (Kaliméra) - Good morning
- Καλησπέρα (Kalispéra) - Good evening
- Καλη νύχτα (Kalí nichta) - Good night
- Αντίο (Αντίο) - Goodbye
- Παρακαλώ (Parakalo) - Please
- Ευχαριστώ (Efcharistó) - Thank you
- Σας ευχαριστώ πολύ (Sas efcharistó polí) - Thank you very much
- Όχι (Óchi) - No
- Ναι (Ne) - Yes
- Συγγνώμη (Syggnómi) - Excuse me
- Δεν καταλαβαίνω (Den katalavéno) - I don't understand
- Μιλάτε Αγγλικά; (Miláte Angliká?) - Do you speak English?

Getting Around:

- Πού είναι η ...; (Pou ine i ... ?) - Where is the ...? (e.g., η παραλία - i paralia - the beach)
- Πόσο κάνει; (Póso kanei?) - How much is it?
- Θέλω να πάω ... (Thelo na páo ...) - I want to go to ...

At the Restaurant:

- Έχετε ...; (Échete ... ?) - Do you have ...? (e.g., ψάρι - psári - fish)
- Το λογαριασμό, παρακαλώ (To logariastmó, parakalo) - The bill, please
- Μπορώ να έχω τον κατάλογο; (Mporó na écho ton katálogo?) - Can I have the menu, please?

Other Useful Phrases:

- Νομίζω (Nomízo) - I think
- Χρειάζομαι βοήθεια (Chriázome voítheia) - I need help
- Σας παρακαλώ, βοηθήστε με (Sas parakalo, voithiste me) - Please help me
- Καλό ταξίδι (Kaló taxídi) - Have a good trip!

Tips:

- Pronunciation is key in Greek. While perfect pronunciation isn't essential, a little effort goes a long way.
- Many Greek words have accents. These accents can change the pronunciation of the word, so it may be helpful to familiarize yourself with them beforehand.

- A smile and kind gesture can often bridge any language gap.
- There are many great Greek phrasebook apps available that can help you with pronunciation and basic phrases.

By learning a few basic phrases, you'll be able to navigate Skiathos with confidence and connect with the warm hospitality of the Greek people.

Chapter 3. Accommodations

3.1. Types of Accommodations

Skiathos offers a diverse range of accommodations to suit every taste and budget. Whether you crave a luxurious beachfront resort or a charming, family-run studio, you'll find the perfect place to unwind and call home during your island escape. Here's a breakdown of the most common types of accommodations in Skiathos:

Luxury Hotels and Resorts:

- Pamper yourself in opulent surroundings with stunning sea views.
- Expect top-notch amenities like infinity pools, spa treatments, a variety of restaurants, and impeccable service.
- Ideal for those seeking an indulgent and carefree vacation experience.

Boutique Hotels:

- Immerse yourself in a stylish and intimate atmosphere with personalized service.
- Often located in the heart of Skiathos Town or picturesque villages, offering easy access to shops and restaurants.

- Perfect for couples or solo travelers seeking a unique and charming stay.

Hotels and Apartments:

- A broad category offering a range of options from budget-friendly to mid-range.
- Many hotels provide amenities like swimming pools, bars, and breakfast buffets.
- Apartments offer a more independent stay with self-catering facilities, ideal for families or longer stays.

Studios and Rooms:

- A cost-effective choice for budget-conscious travelers.
- Typically basic with a sleeping area, bathroom, and sometimes a balcony.
- Often located in central locations or close to beaches, perfect for those who plan to spend most of their time exploring.

Villas and Vacation Rentals:

- Ideal for families, groups, or those seeking privacy and space.
- Villas offer luxurious amenities like private pools, gardens, and stunning views.

- Vacation rentals can range from charming apartments to standalone houses, providing a more homey feel.

Consider These Factors When Choosing Your Accommodation:

- **Location:** Do you want to be in the heart of the action or prefer a quieter, more secluded spot?
- **Budget:** Skiathos caters to different budgets, so decide how much you're comfortable spending per night.
- **Travel Style:** Are you seeking luxury, a social atmosphere, or a more independent stay?
- **Amenities:** Prioritize the features that are important to you, such as a pool, balcony, or proximity to the beach.

Tips for Booking Your Stay:

- **Book in advance:** Skiathos is a popular destination, especially during peak season.
- **Research online:** Read reviews and compare prices on travel booking websites and local accommodation websites.

- **Consider contacting accommodation directly:** You might score a better deal or have specific requests addressed.

With its diverse range of accommodations, Skiathos offers the perfect place to rest, relax, and create lasting memories during your Greek island adventure.

3.2. Top Hotels for Couples

Here's a guide to some of the top hotels that will set the stage for an unforgettable couple's getaway:

Luxury Escape:

- **Elivi Skiathos:** This posh seaside resort offers a zen atmosphere with multiple pools, a world-class spa, and three restaurants. Perfect for pampering yourselves and indulging in culinary delights.
- **Kassandra Bay Resort, Suites & Spa:** Upscale and stylish, this resort boasts sleek suites, private beach access, and a serene spa. Ideal for those who crave a luxurious and relaxing retreat.

Secluded Serenity:

- **Mandraki Village Boutique Hotel:** This adults-only haven features beautiful gardens, a charming pool area, and tranquil rooms. Escape the crowds and enjoy intimate moments amidst the idyllic setting.
- **Villa Yiannis (Adult Friendly):** Another gem for adults-only escapes, offering self-catering studios with breathtaking views of the Aegean Sea and Strofilia Lake. Ideal for couples seeking a romantic hideaway with stunning scenery.

Romantic Ambiance:

- **Atrium Hotel:** This hotel boasts breathtaking views and impeccable service, creating a truly blissful escape. Perfect for couples who appreciate stunning vistas and attentive hospitality.
- **La Luna Hotel:** Soak in the intimate atmosphere and personalized service at La Luna Hotel. Charming and romantic, it's ideal for those seeking a cozy and unforgettable getaway.

Budget-Friendly Charm:

- **Skiathos House:** This charming hotel offers a romantic ambiance at a more affordable price point. Located in Skiathos Town, it provides a great location for exploring the island's heart.
- **Villa Melia:** This option allows you to experience the feel of a luxurious villa without breaking the bank. Perfect for couples seeking a private and romantic escape with a touch of Greek charm.

Remember: Consider your priorities when choosing a hotel. Do you crave ultimate luxury, a secluded escape, or a charming and romantic ambiance? Think about the experiences you want to have as a couple and choose a hotel that complements your vision.

Bonus Tip: Many hotels offer special couple's packages that might include extras like spa treatments, champagne breakfasts, or romantic dinner reservations. Explore these options to add a touch of magic to your stay!

3.3. Family-Friendly Resorts

Skiathos isn't just a haven for couples and romantic getaways. This vibrant island offers a delightful experience for families as well. Here's a look at some of Skiathos' top resorts that cater to families, ensuring a memorable vacation for all ages:

Upscale Luxury with Kid-Friendly Fun:

- **Elivi Skiathos:** Nestled on the famed Koukounaries Bay, Elivi Skiathos boasts a zen-like atmosphere with a focus on family fun. Two outdoor pools, including a dedicated children's pool, keep the little ones entertained. A kids' club offers supervised activities, while parents can relax by the pool or indulge in the on-site spa.
- **Kassandra Bay Resort, Suites & Spa:** This upscale resort offers a luxurious experience with a family-friendly twist. Two sparkling pools, one with a children's section, provide endless splashy fun. A dedicated kids' club keeps younger guests entertained, while a private beach area allows for carefree relaxation.

Comfort and Convenience for the Whole Family:

- **Skiathos Princess Resort:** This expansive resort offers spacious rooms, ideal for families. With a dedicated children's pool, playground, and kids' club, it caters to all ages. Parents can enjoy a variety of water sports, tennis courts, or simply unwind by the poolside.

A Touch of Tradition with Family Flair:

- **Mandraki Village Boutique Hotel:** This charming hotel offers a taste of traditional Greek hospitality. While not a large resort, it provides a family-friendly atmosphere with a children's pool and playground. Its location near Skiathos Town allows families to explore the island's vibrant heart.

Considerations When Choosing:

- **Age of your children:** Resorts with dedicated kids' clubs and organized activities are ideal for older children. Younger children might be happier with a smaller pool and a more relaxed atmosphere.
- **Location:** Beachfront resorts offer easy access to the water, while those closer to

town provide a chance to explore Skiathos' charming streets and shops.
- **Budget:** Luxury resorts offer a wider range of amenities but come at a premium price. Smaller, family-run hotels provide a cozy atmosphere at a more affordable rate.

Beyond the Resort:

Don't forget to explore Skiathos' family-friendly offerings outside the resort. Boat trips to secluded beaches, exploring hidden coves, and enjoying delicious meals at tavernas with outdoor seating will create lasting memories for the whole family.

By choosing the right resort and venturing out to explore the island's charm, your Skiathos family vacation is sure to be an unforgettable adventure.

3.4. Budget Stays for Solo Travelers

Skiathos isn't just for couples and honeymooners! Solo travelers can experience the island's magic too, and on a budget. Here are some fantastic options for affordable stays that cater to the independent adventurer:

Hostels and Budget-Friendly Hotels:

- Hostels: Skiathos offers a couple of lively hostels perfect for meeting fellow travelers. You'll find dorm rooms for the most budget-conscious adventurer, and some offer private rooms at a reasonable price. Social events and tours are often organized, making it a great way to connect with others.
- Budget Hotels: Several small, family-run hotels offer clean, comfortable rooms at affordable rates. Look outside the main town center for slightly cheaper options. Many provide basic amenities like breakfast and balconies, perfect for enjoying your morning coffee.

Studios and Apartments:

- Studios: Studios are a fantastic option for solo travelers, offering a private space with a kitchenette or cooking facilities. This flexibility allows you to prepare some meals and save on dining expenses. Look for studios in quieter areas or slightly away from the main beaches for the best deals.
- Apartments: Sharing an apartment with another solo traveler you meet on the island can be a cost-effective option. Platforms like

Airbnb or local listing websites often have apartment listings perfect for budget-minded travelers.

Tips for Saving on Accommodation:

- **Travel in the Shoulder Seasons:** Consider visiting Skiathos in the shoulder seasons (April-May or September-October) to avoid peak season prices. You'll still enjoy warm weather and smaller crowds.
- **Book in Advance, Especially for Studios:** Popular studios get booked quickly, so plan your trip and secure your accommodation in advance, especially during the peak summer months.
- **Consider Location:** While beachfront locations are tempting, explore options slightly inland or further from the main town for significant savings. The island is small, and local buses are readily available for exploring different areas.

Alternative Stays:

- **Camping:** For the truly adventurous soul, consider camping! There are a couple of campsites on the island offering a budget-friendly and unique way to experience Skiathos' natural beauty.

Remember:

Solo travel is an enriching experience, and Skiathos offers a welcoming atmosphere for independent explorers. With a little planning and these budget-friendly options, you can find the perfect stay for your solo adventure!

Chapter 4. Getting Around

4.1. Public Transportation

Skiathos boasts a convenient and affordable public transportation system, perfect for exploring the island without needing to rent a car. Here's what you need to know to navigate Skiathos like a local:

Buses:

- **The Network:** Skiathos has a well-connected bus network operated by Skiathos Transports. Modern, air-conditioned white buses run frequently throughout the day, connecting Skiathos Town with popular destinations like Koukounaries Beach, the airport, and various beaches along the south coast. There's also a separate company with older green buses running similar routes.
- **Fares:** Ticket prices depend on the distance you travel. Generally, fares are either €2 or €3 one way. Fares are usually paid directly on the bus to the conductor.
- **Benefits:** Taking the bus is a budget-friendly and scenic way to explore the island. You can hop off at different

beaches, soak in the views, and experience the local vibe.

Taxis:

- Taxis are readily available in Skiathos Town and at designated taxi ranks around the island. They can be a convenient option, especially with luggage or for late-night travel. Fares are metered, so you'll only pay for the distance traveled.

Water Taxis:

- While not a primary mode of public transportation, water taxis offer a unique way to travel between Skiathos Town and some beaches and nearby islands like Skopelos. These are typically private services, so arrange your transfer and inquire about fares in advance.

Tips for Using Public Transportation:

- Bus schedules are usually displayed at bus stops, although they may vary depending on the season. Consider asking your hotel or accommodation for the latest timetable.
- Validate your bus ticket upon boarding by stamping it in the machine provided.

- Download a map of Skiathos bus routes to plan your journeys effectively.
- Be prepared for a bit of spontaneity - buses in Greece might not always run according to a strict schedule. Embrace the relaxed island atmosphere!

Alternative Ways to Get Around:

- **Bicycles:** Renting a bike is a fun and active way to explore the island at your own pace. Several shops offer bike rentals in Skiathos Town.
- **Scooters/Motorbikes:** For the more adventurous traveler, renting a scooter or motorbike allows for greater flexibility and exploration of off-the-beaten-path locations. Remember to have a valid driver's license and wear a helmet.

By utilizing public transportation or alternative options, you can discover the charm of Skiathos without needing to rent a car. So, ditch the car rental hassle, and embrace the laid-back island way of life!

4.2. Car Rentals

With a rental car, you can unlock the island's hidden gems, charming villages nestled in the hills, and secluded coves accessible only by road. Here's what you need to know about car rentals in Skiathos:

The Perks of Having Wheels:

- **Freedom and Flexibility:** Explore Skiathos at your own pace, following your itinerary and discovering off-the-beaten-path locations.
- **Beach Hopping Bliss:** Visit a different beach each day, from the lively stretches to hidden, secluded bays.
- **Village Vibes:** Venture beyond the main tourist areas and discover the character and charm of traditional Skiathos villages.
- **Scenic Drives:** Take in breathtaking panoramic views on scenic coastal roads.

Renting Made Easy:

- **Location, Location, Location:** Rental agencies are plentiful, with options at Skiathos International Airport, the main port, and in Skiathos Town.

- **Variety is Key:** Choose from international car rental companies like Budget, Avis, and Hertz, or discover local Skiathos agencies that might offer more personalized service.
- **Book Ahead:** Especially during peak season (July and August), consider booking your car rental in advance to secure the type of vehicle you desire.

What to Consider:

- **Car Size:** Small, fuel-efficient vehicles are ideal for navigating narrow island roads and finding parking in town centers.
- **Automatic vs. Manual:** Automatic transmission might be easier, especially for navigating unfamiliar roads with potential switchbacks.
- **Insurance:** While basic insurance is usually included, consider additional coverage for peace of mind.
- **Fuel Policy:** Many rentals opt for a full-to-full fuel policy, so plan to refill the tank before returning the car.
- **International Driver's Permit:** While not always mandatory, an International Driver's Permit (IDP) is recommended, especially if renting from a local agency.

Local Tips:

- **Price Comparison:** Compare rates from different rental agencies to find the best deal.
- **Read the Fine Print:** Before finalizing your rental, carefully review the contract, including any additional fees or limitations.
- **Parking:** Parking can be limited in some areas, especially during peak season. Be mindful of designated parking zones and avoid blocking traffic.

With a little planning and these handy tips, renting a car in Skiathos can be a smooth and rewarding experience. Buckle up and get ready to discover the hidden treasures of this beautiful island!

4.3. Biking and Walking

Skiathos isn't just about sprawling beaches and turquoise waters. Lace up your walking shoes or hop on a bike to discover the island's hidden gems, charming villages, and stunning natural beauty.

Calling all Cyclists:

- **Cycle the Coastlines:** Skiathos boasts a network of paved coastal roads perfect for scenic cycling adventures.Explore the southern route that winds past idyllic beaches like Koukounaries, Banana, and Small Banana. The northern route offers a more challenging terrain with breathtaking views from high points.
- **Mountain Majesty:** For experienced cyclists, Skiathos offers a range of mountain bike trails. Explore the inland areas, discover hidden monasteries like Evangelistria and Agios Charalambos, and conquer the rewarding climb to Mytikas Peak for panoramic island vistas.
- **Bike Rentals:** Numerous shops around the island offer rentals for various types of bicycles, including mountain bikes, hybrids, and easy-riding cruisers.

Hitting the Trails:

- **Walking Wonders:** Skiathos is a walker's paradise with nearly 200 kilometers of well-maintained trails. Embark on an easy stroll through the pine forests near Koukounaries Beach or challenge yourself

with the moderate hike to the scenic Kastro viewpoint overlooking the old town.
- **Waterside Wanderings:** Lace up your walking shoes and explore the coastal paths that connect many of Skiathos' beautiful beaches. Discover hidden coves, witness dramatic rock formations, and stumble upon charming tavernas along the way.
- **Village Vibes:** Meander through the narrow alleys of Skiathos Town, exploring its neoclassical architecture, historical landmarks like the Papadiamantis House Museum, and the charming harbor area. Take a walk to the charming village of Hora with its traditional tavernas and windmill.

Tips for Bikers and Walkers:

- **Hydration is Key:** Pack plenty of water, especially during the hot summer months.
- **Sun Smarts:** Apply sunscreen regularly and wear a hat to protect yourself from the strong Greek sun.
- **Mind the Terrain:** Wear appropriate footwear for your chosen activity. Opt for sturdy walking shoes or hiking boots for uneven terrain and sandals or light shoes for coastal walks.

- **Explore Responsibly:** Respect the local environment, stay on designated trails, and dispose of any waste properly.
- **Embrace the Journey:** Take your time, soak in the scenery, and enjoy the relaxed pace of island life.

Whether you're a cycling enthusiast or a passionate walker, Skiathos offers a wealth of opportunities to discover the island beyond the beach. So lace up your shoes, grab your bike (or rent one), and get ready for an unforgettable adventure!

Chapter 5. Exploring Skiathos

5.1. Main Attractions

Skiathos isn't just a postcard-perfect island; it's a treasure trove of experiences waiting to be discovered. Here's a glimpse into the island's top attractions that will leave you breathless:

Beach Bliss:

- **Koukounaries Beach:** Often hailed as one of Greece's most stunning beaches, Koukounaries boasts golden sand, turquoise waters, and a lush pine forest reaching right up to the shore. Perfect for swimming, sunbathing, and water sports.
- **Lalaria Beach:** Accessible only by boat, Lalaria is a secluded cove famous for its dramatic white rock formations, crystal-clear waters, and idyllic atmosphere. Ideal for those seeking a tranquil escape.
- **Banana Beach:** As the name suggests, Banana Beach offers a unique curved bay with golden sand and shallow waters, perfect for families with young children. Enjoy water sports, sun loungers, and beach bars.

- **Numerous Hidden Coves:** Explore the island's coastline and discover hidden coves like Small Banana, Agia Eleni, and Mikro Aselinos. Each offers a unique charm, perfect for a relaxed beach day.

Historical Gems:

- **Medieval Castle:** Perched on a rocky peninsula overlooking the harbor, the Venetian castle offers a glimpse into Skiathos's past. Explore the ramparts, remnants of houses, and captivating views.
- **Monastery of Evangelistria:** Nestled amidst pine trees, this 18th-century monastery is a beautiful example of Byzantine architecture. Admire the frescoes, religious icons, and panoramic island views.
- **Skiathos Town:** Wander the charming streets lined with whitewashed houses, colorful shops, and traditional tavernas. Explore the Papadiamantis House, a museum dedicated to the famous Greek author.

Natural Wonders:

- **Boat Tours:** Embark on a boat tour to discover hidden coves, sea caves, and

secluded beaches inaccessible by land.Witness the island's dramatic coastline from a different perspective.
- **Hiking Trails:** Lace up your walking shoes and explore the island's network of well-maintained trails. Hike through forests, past quaint villages, and be rewarded with breathtaking panoramas.
- **Scuba Diving and Snorkeling:** Explore the underwater world teeming with colorful marine life. Crystal-clear waters and hidden coves provide a paradise for diving enthusiasts.

Beyond the Beach:

- **Nightlife:** Skiathos transforms at night with vibrant bars and clubs lining the harbor. Enjoy live music, delicious cocktails, and a taste of the island's energetic nightlife scene.
- **Foodie Delights:** Savor fresh seafood, local delicacies, and traditional Greek cuisine at tavernas and restaurants.Don't miss out on the chance to indulge in Skiathos's culinary delights.

This is just a taste of the magic that awaits in Skiathos. With its diverse offerings, this island paradise caters to every kind of traveler. So, pack your bags and get ready to discover your own slice of heaven!

5.2. Hidden Gems

Skiathos isn't just about sunbeds and sparkling waters (although those are pretty amazing too!). This island boasts a treasure trove of hidden gems waiting to be discovered by curious travelers. Here are a few off-the-beaten-path experiences to add a touch of magic to your Skiathos adventure:

- **Kastro & Kastro Beach:** Take a historical hike to the ruins of Kastro, the island's ancient settlement perched on a dramatic clifftop. Explore the remnants of the Byzantine castle and soak in the panoramic views before descending a scenic path to discover Kastro Beach, a secluded cove with crystal-clear waters.
- **Evangelistria Church:** Delve into Skiathos' rich history at Evangelistria Church, where the first Greek flag was reportedly blessed in the 18th century. Admire the beautiful architecture and immerse yourself in the island's patriotic spirit.

- **Walking Trails:** Lace up your walking shoes and explore Skiathos' scenic network of trails. Venture through lush olive groves, encounter hidden chapels, and stumble upon breathtaking viewpoints offering a glimpse of the island's natural beauty.
- **Bourtzi Peninsula:** Just a short stroll from the harbor lies Bourtzi, a small pine-covered peninsula steeped in history. Explore the ruins of an old fortress and wander through charming gardens, offering a peaceful escape from the summertime crowds.
- **Sailing Adventures:** Embark on a sailing adventure and discover hidden coves and secluded beaches inaccessible by land. Unwind on pristine sands, snorkel in crystal-clear waters, and explore the island's coastline from a unique perspective.
- **Local Tavernas:** Venture beyond the main tourist strip and discover hidden tavernas tucked away in charming villages. Savor delicious local cuisine prepared with fresh, seasonal ingredients, and experience the warmth of Greek hospitality.
- **Papadiamantis House:** Literature buffs can pay homage to Alexandros Papadiamantis, a famous Greek writer, by

visiting his former residence. Now a museum, the house offers a glimpse into his life and works.

Remember: Part of the charm of hidden gems is the element of discovery. Engage with locals, ask for recommendations,and keep your eyes peeled for tucked-away treasures. With a sense of adventure, you'll be sure to unearth your own unique Skiathos experiences.

5.3. Beaches

Skiathos boasts over 60 beaches, each offering a unique charm. From long stretches of golden sand to secluded coves and dramatic rock formations, there's a perfect beach paradise waiting for every visitor. Here's a glimpse into some of Skiathos's most beloved beaches:

The A-List Beaches:

- **Koukounaries Beach:** This iconic beach is a must-visit. Imagine soft, golden sand backed by a lush pine forest,with crystal-clear turquoise waters lapping at the shore. Sunbeds and water sports are

available, making it ideal for families and relaxation seekers alike.
- **Lalaria Beach:** This dramatic beach features white pebbles and unique rock formations, including the famous "Troulos" (dome) carved by the sea. Accessible only by boat, Lalaria offers a breathtaking and secluded escape.
- **Banana Beach:** As the name suggests, this beach is shaped like a banana and is known for its calm waters and relaxed atmosphere. Perfect for swimming, snorkeling, or simply soaking up the sun.

Hidden Gems:

- **Kolios Beach:** This secluded beach offers a haven of tranquility. Surrounded by pine trees and olive groves, it's ideal for those seeking a peaceful escape.
- **Mandraki Beach:** This long stretch of golden sand boasts stunning views of Mount Pelion and offers a relaxed atmosphere with a beach bar for refreshments.
- **Tsougria Island Beaches:** Take a boat trip to Tsougria, a small, uninhabited island with several stunning beaches.Explore secluded coves with crystal-clear waters and bask in the serenity of this natural paradise.

Choosing Your Beach:

With so many options, here's how to pick your perfect beach:

- **Family Fun:** Koukounaries, Banana, and Troulos beaches offer shallow waters, amenities, and a relaxed vibe, perfect for families.
- **Water Sports:** Banana, Koukounaries, and Megalos Aselinos beaches offer windsurfing, jet skiing, and other water sports.
- **Seclusion:** Kolios, Maratha, and some coves on Tsougria island offer a peaceful escape for those seeking tranquility.
- **Dramatic Scenery:** Lalaria beach with its rock formations and some of the beaches on the eastern coast provide a more dramatic landscape.

Beyond the Beach:

Many beaches have tavernas serving delicious Greek cuisine and refreshing drinks. Beach vendors often rent sunbeds and umbrellas for a comfortable beach day.

Remember:

- Research the beaches beforehand to find the ones that suit your interests.
- Pack essentials like sunscreen, water, and a hat for a carefree beach experience.
- Many beaches are accessible by car or bus, while others require boat trips.

Get ready to dive into the turquoise waters, sink your toes into the soft sand, and discover your own slice of paradise on the beaches of Skiathos!

5.4. Historical Sites and Museums

Beyond the postcard-perfect beaches, Skiathos boasts a rich history waiting to be explored. Immerse yourself in the island's captivating past by visiting these historical sites and museums:

Museums:

- **The Papadiamantis House:** Step back in time and explore the former residence of Alexandros Papadiamantis, a renowned Greek novelist. This museum offers a glimpse into his life and work, showcasing his personal belongings and manuscripts alongside traditional Skiathian folk objects.

- **Skiathitiko Spiti (Skiathos House):** Delve into the traditional way of life on Skiathos at this charming museum. Housed in a restored 19th-century captain's mansion, exhibits depict island life through the ages, featuring domestic utensils, furniture, and local costumes.
- **Museum of Naval & Cultural Tradition of Skiathos:** Embark on a maritime adventure at this museum dedicated to Skiathos's long and proud naval history. Explore exhibits showcasing ship models, nautical instruments, and artifacts that tell the story of the island's seafaring heritage.

Historical Sites:

- **Monastery of Panagia Evangelistria:** Perched atop a hill overlooking the island, this 18th-century monastery offers breathtaking panoramic views. Explore the beautifully preserved church and its surrounding buildings, and don't miss the surprisingly well-curated museum collection housed within the monastery walls.
- **Kastro (Castle):** The remnants of the Venetian castle, perched on a small peninsula near the harbor, offer a glimpse into Skiathos's role as a defensive outpost

during medieval times. Explore the ruins and soak in the stunning sea views.
- **Old Town:** Wander through the charming alleys of Skiathos Town, a maze of whitewashed houses, traditional tavernas, and hidden courtyards. Many of the buildings boast neoclassical architecture, remnants of the island's prosperous past.

Exploring Further:

For history buffs, consider venturing beyond the main town. Several historical churches and monasteries are scattered across the island, each with their own unique story to tell. Additionally, boat trips can be arranged to visit nearby islands with significant historical sites, such as Skopelos, where scenes from the movie "Mamma Mia!" were filmed.

Tips:

- Purchase a combined ticket for entry to several museums for a more economical visit.
- Most museums have designated opening hours, so plan your visits accordingly.
- Dress modestly when visiting monasteries and religious sites.

- Many historical sites offer stunning views, so don't forget your camera!

By incorporating historical and cultural experiences into your itinerary, you'll gain a deeper appreciation for the rich tapestry that makes Skiathos such a captivating destination.

5.5. *Natural Wonders and Hiking Trails*

Beyond the postcard-perfect beaches, Skiathos boasts a verdant heart waiting to be explored. Lace up your hiking boots and immerse yourself in the island's natural beauty with these trails and wonders:

Hiking Trails:

- **The Kastro Trail:** This moderate trail leads to the imposing medieval fortress perched on the island's highest point. Enjoy panoramic views and delve into Skiathos' rich history.
- **The Monastery of Evangelistria Trail:** A scenic route through pine forests and olive groves, culminating in the charming Evangelistria Monastery. Take in

breathtaking sea vistas and discover the island's spiritual side.

- **The Limnonari to Banana Beach Trail:** A leisurely path along the stunning Skiathos coastline, connecting two picturesque beaches. Perfect for a refreshing swim and soaking up the Aegean sunshine.
- **The Kalamaki to Lalaria Trail:** A more challenging hike with rewarding views. Traverse through diverse landscapes, encountering hidden coves and dramatic rock formations.

Natural Wonders:

- **Drakon Osera (Dragon's Bay):** A secluded cove accessible only by foot or boat. Believed by some to resemble a dragon's silhouette, this pristine beach offers tranquility and crystal-clear waters.
- **The Blue Hole:** A hidden gem near Xenia Beach. This natural wonder features a captivating rock pool with mesmerizing turquoise waters, perfect for a refreshing dip.
- **The Lalaria Beach:** Famous for its unique, whitewashed pebbles, Lalaria Beach is a natural marvel. Explore the dramatic rock formations and coves for a truly unforgettable experience.

Tips for Hikers:

- **Start your hikes early** to avoid the midday heat.
- **Bring plenty of water** and stay hydrated throughout your trek.
- **Wear proper footwear** with good grip for uneven terrain.
- **Pack sun protection,** a hat, and sunglasses.
- **Be mindful of the environment** and leave no trace behind.
- **Let someone know your hiking plans** and estimated return time.

Embrace the adventure and discover the hidden beauty of Skiathos. With a bit of planning and these suggestions, you're sure to have an unforgettable experience exploring the island's natural wonders.

Chapter 6. Activities and Adventures

6.1. Water Sports

Skiathos isn't just a beach destination; it's a playground for water enthusiasts! With its turquoise waters and sheltered coves, the island offers a thrilling array of water sports to suit every level of experience.

For the Adrenaline Junkie:

- **Jet Skiing:** Carve through the waves and feel the rush of adrenaline as you zip around the coastline.
- **Parasailing:** Soar high above the water and take in breathtaking views of Skiathos and neighboring islands.
- **Windsurfing and Kitesurfing:** Harness the power of the wind and test your skills on the waves (lessons are available for beginners).
- **Wakeboarding and Waterskiing:** Get towed behind a boat and experience the exhilaration of gliding across the water.

For a Fun-Filled Day:

- **Towable Rides:** Hold on tight and scream with delight as you're pulled along on tubes, sofas, or rings behind a boat.
- **Stand Up Paddling (SUP):** Explore hidden coves and enjoy a scenic paddle at your own pace. Great for all fitness levels.
- **Kayaking or Canoeing:** Paddle along the coastline, discover secluded beaches, and spot marine life in crystal-clear waters.
- **Snorkeling and Scuba Diving:** Immerse yourself in the underwater world and discover the vibrant marine life thriving in Skiathos' reefs.

Relax and Reflect:

- **Boat Tours:** Embark on a guided boat tour and discover hidden coves, secluded beaches, and historical landmarks.
- **Sailing:** Charter a sailboat and set sail on a romantic sunset cruise or a fun-filled day trip exploring the island's coastline.
- **Sea Kayaking:** Paddle along the scenic coastline and enjoy a peaceful exploration of hidden coves and secluded beaches.

Tips for Booking Water Sports:

- Numerous water sports operators are located on the beaches of Skiathos.
- Prices can vary depending on the activity and duration.
- Booking in advance, especially during peak season, is recommended.
- Many operators offer packages that combine different activities.
- Always prioritize safety and choose a reputable operator with qualified instructors.

Remember: Don't forget your swimsuit, sunscreen, sunglasses, and a hat for a day of aquatic adventure!

6.2. Boat Tours and Island Hopping

The sparkling Aegean Sea beckons beyond the shores of Skiathos, and what better way to discover its hidden coves and neighboring islands than with a thrilling boat tour or adventurous island hopping escapade? Here's your guide to exploring the turquoise waters around Skiathos:

Boat Tours:

- **Around the Island:** Embark on a scenic journey around Skiathos, marveling at hidden beaches, dramatic rock formations, and secluded coves. These tours often include swimming stops at pristine locations and glimpses of marine life.
- **Secluded Beach Escape:** Escape the crowds and discover untouched beauty with a boat tour to isolated beaches accessible only by water. Imagine yourself basking on a pristine stretch of sand with nothing but the sound of waves and the call of seabirds.
- **Sunset Cruises:** Paint your memories with vibrant hues as you set sail on a sunset cruise. Witness the sky ablaze with color as the sun dips below the horizon, creating a truly unforgettable experience.

Island Hopping Adventures:

- **Skopelos and Alonissos:** Discover the neighboring islands of Skopelos, famous for its Mamma Mia filming locations, and Alonissos, a haven for marine life and boasting stunning beaches. These tours typically include guided exploration time on each island.
- **Smaller Island Gems:** Explore the charm of smaller islands near Skiathos, such as

Tsougria with its traditional village and crystal-clear waters, or Tis Dyo Adelfes (Two Sisters), a tiny islet known for its unique rock formations.

Choosing Your Boat Tour:

- **Style:** Decide on your preferred vessel - a traditional wooden boat offers a charming experience, while a modern catamaran ensures speed and comfort.
- **Duration:** Opt for a half-day tour for a taste of exploration, or a full-day adventure for a more immersive experience.
- **Inclusions:** Consider tours with meals included for convenience, or choose one focused solely on the sailing experience and pack your own snacks.

Top Tips:

- Book your boat tour in advance, especially during peak season.
- Pack sunscreen, sunglasses, a hat, and a swimsuit for swimming stops.
- Bring cash for any additional purchases onboard or at island stops.
- Be aware of potential seasickness and carry medication if needed.

Embrace the island vibes, feel the salty breeze in your hair, and discover hidden gems with a Skiathos boat tour or island hopping adventure. It's an experience that will leave you breathless and yearning for more.

6.3. Hiking and Nature Walks

Beyond the idyllic beaches, Skiathos boasts a hidden gem: a network of hiking trails that weave through its lush interior. Whether you're a seasoned hiker or a casual nature enthusiast, Skiathos has paths to suit all abilities, offering a chance to:

- **Uncover hidden coves and secluded beaches:** Many trails lead to lesser-known beaches, perfect for escaping the crowds and finding your own slice of paradise.
- **Immerse yourself in nature:** Breathe in the fresh pine-scented air as you traverse rolling hills, encounter vibrant wildflowers, and spot local birdlife.
- **Discover historical and cultural treasures:** Stumble upon ancient ruins, charming monasteries nestled amidst the hills, and traditional villages that offer a glimpse into Skiathos' rich heritage.

- **Enjoy panoramic vistas:** Challenge yourself with a moderate hike and be rewarded with breathtaking views of the Aegean Sea, neighboring islands, and the dramatic coastline.

Hitting the Trails:

Here's a taste of what Skiathos' hiking trails offer:

- **For the Leisurely Explorer:** The easy **Skiathos Town Circular** allows you to explore the charming capital at your own pace, taking in historical sites and enjoying harbor views.
- **For the Beach Lover:** The **Koukounaries Beach Loop** combines a walk through the famed pine forest with visits to stunning beaches like Agistros and Gournes.
- **For the History Buff:** The **Evangelistria Monastery - Agios Charalambos Monastery - Kastro Beach** route combines a historical pilgrimage with a rewarding coastal finale.

Tips for Hikers:

- **Plan ahead:** Research trails that suit your fitness level and interests. Purchase a hiking map or download a GPS app to navigate the trails.
- **Embrace the elements:** Pack sun protection, a hat, comfortable shoes, and plenty of water, especially during the hot summer months.
- **Respect the environment:** Stay on designated trails, avoid disturbing wildlife, and pack out all your trash.

Finding Guided Hikes:

For those who prefer a guided experience, several local companies offer organized hikes with knowledgeable guides who can share insights about the island's flora, fauna, and history.

So lace up your boots, grab your hat, and get ready to explore the wild beauty of Skiathos!

6.4. Cultural Activities and Workshops

Beyond the idyllic beaches, Skiathos offers a treasure trove of cultural experiences waiting to be explored. Here's how you can delve deeper into the island's rich heritage and artistic spirit:

Unveil Local Traditions:

- **Folklore Shows:** Immerse yourself in the vibrant energy of a traditional Greek night. Witness energetic dances, captivating music, and colorful costumes that bring Skiathos' folklore to life.
- **Museum Explorations:** Step back in time at the **Skiathos Town Museum**, housing archaeological finds, historical artifacts, and exhibits showcasing the island's past. The **Folklore Museum** delves into local customs and traditions, offering a glimpse into the lives of past generations.
- **Pottery Workshops:** Unleash your inner artist at a pottery workshop. Learn the craft of shaping clay from local artisans and create your own ceramic masterpiece to take home as a unique souvenir.

Embrace the Creative Spirit:

- **The Skiathos Garden Theatre:** Nestled amidst lush greenery, this open-air theatre stages a variety of cultural events throughout the summer. Catch captivating dance

performances, soulful music evenings, or artistic workshops – all against the backdrop of the Aegean Sea.
- **Cooking Classes:** Learn the secrets of Skiathos cuisine by taking a cooking class. Discover the art of preparing fresh, local ingredients and traditional dishes under the guidance of experienced chefs.
- **Sailing Workshops:** Embark on a unique learning experience with a sailing workshop. Gain basic sailing skills or hone your existing knowledge while navigating the crystal-clear waters surrounding Skiathos.

Festivals and Events:

- **Skiathos International Film Festival:** Held annually in September, this festival showcases independent films from around the world, offering screenings under the stars and opportunities to mingle with filmmakers.
- **Religious Festivals:** Immerse yourself in the local spirit by attending a vibrant religious festival. Witness colorful processions, cultural performances, and a deep connection to the island's faith. (Specific dates vary, so check local listings for upcoming events).

Insider Tip:

- Look out for local artisans selling handmade jewelry, pottery, and other traditional crafts at shops and open-air markets. These treasures make for authentic souvenirs and support the local community.

By participating in these cultural activities and workshops, you'll gain a deeper appreciation for Skiathos' rich tapestry beyond the postcard-perfect beaches. So, pack your curiosity and get ready for a truly enriching island experience!

6.5. Nightlife and Entertainment

Skiathos isn't just about sun-kissed days; it transforms into a vibrant hub of nightlife after dark. Whether you crave pulsating dance floors or relaxed evenings with live music, Skiathos caters to all tastes. Here's your guide to experiencing the best of Skiathos' after-hours scene:

Harbour Lights and Club Scene:

- **Skiathos Town**: The beating heart of Skiathos nightlife is concentrated around the picturesque harbour. Bars like **Jaguar** and

Montecristo boast trendy settings, live DJs, and energetic crowds. Dress up and prepare to dance the night away!
- **Club hopping**: For the ultimate clubbing experience, head to the **Old Port** area. Several clubs like **BBC** and **Paradise** offer open-air terraces, pulsating music, and late-night revelry.

Beyond the Dance Floor:

- **Cocktail Bars**: If you prefer a more relaxed vibe, explore the charming backstreets of Skiathos Town. Hidden courtyards host stylish cocktail bars like **Anderssons** and **The Alchemist**, perfect for enjoying handcrafted drinks and conversation.
- **Live Music**: Immerse yourself in the local spirit at tavernas and bars that showcase live Greek music. Danny & Zoe's Blind Dog is a local favorite, offering a laid-back atmosphere and talented musicians.
- **Beach Bars**: For a taste of paradise under the stars, head to **Banana Beach**. This iconic beach bar offers sunset cocktails, live DJ sets, and a carefree atmosphere perfect for soaking up the island vibes.

Tips for a Memorable Night Out:

- **Dress code**: While some clubs have a dress code, most bars and tavernas are casual. Pack a versatile outfit that can transition from day to night.
- **Bar hopping**: Skiathos is compact, making bar hopping a breeze. Explore different areas and discover your favorite spots.
- **Greek Night**: Experience traditional Greek culture at a taverna hosting a Greek night. Enjoy delicious food, live music, and even participate in some traditional dancing!
- **Safety first**: Pace yourself with drinks and be aware of your surroundings, especially late at night.

Remember:

- Nightlife in Skiathos typically gets going later in the evening, around 11 pm onwards.
- Many bars and clubs stay open until the early hours of the morning.
- Taxis are readily available, or take a leisurely stroll back to your hotel along the scenic harbour front.

With its diverse nightlife options, Skiathos guarantees an unforgettable experience for night owls and laid-back revelers alike. So, pack your dancing shoes or your favorite cocktail dress, and prepare to embrace the magic of Skiathos after dark!

Chapter 7. Dining and Cuisine

7.1. Traditional Greek Cuisine

Skiathos isn't just a beach paradise; it's a haven for delicious, fresh Greek cuisine. Here, the Aegean Sea's bounty mingles with the island's agricultural heritage, creating a unique flavor profile unlike any other. Get ready to tantalize your taste buds with these Skiathos specialties:

Seafood Sensations:

- **Fresh Catch:** Skiathos boasts some of the freshest seafood in Greece. Sample grilled octopus, sardines, or local lobster.
- **Fish stews:** Dive into flavorful stews made with local fish varieties like dentex, grouper, and monkfish.
- **Crayfish with "Horta" (wild greens):** A unique Skiathos dish featuring succulent crayfish simmered with seasonal wild greens for a delightful combination of textures and flavors.

Land and Sea Matrimony:

- **"Peskandritsa" Stew:** This hearty stew marries fresh fish with local vegetables and sometimes even goat or lamb, creating a robust and satisfying dish.

From the Farm to Your Table:

- **Skiathos Cheese Pie:** This spiral-shaped pie boasts a savory filling of local cheeses and herbs, a must-try for any cheese lover.
- **"Hortopita":** Wild greens, a staple on Skiathos, are transformed into delicious "hortopita" pies with a flaky filo pastry crust.
- **Fava:** This creamy yellow split pea purée is a classic Greek dish, often served with fresh seafood or fried onions.

Sweet Endings:

- **Skiathos Baklava:** Indulge in a sweeter side of Skiathos with their take on this classic Greek pastry, known for its rich flavor and flaky crust.

Don't Miss:

- **Meze:** Embrace the Greek tradition of "meze," a selection of small plates perfect for sharing. Sample various appetizers, dips, and spreads alongside your favorite local wine or ouzo.

- **Local Wines:** Pair your meal with a glass of wine produced on the island. From crisp whites to robust reds, Skiathos offers a variety to complement your culinary adventure.

Foodie Tips:

- Look for tavernas tucked away in charming villages or lining the waterfront.
- Opt for family-run establishments where recipes are passed down through generations.
- Embrace the seasonality of ingredients – the freshest flavors await!

By venturing beyond the typical tourist fare, you'll discover the true essence of Skiathos cuisine – a delicious harmony between the island's maritime bounty and its rich agricultural heart.

7.2. Best Restaurants for Couples

Skiathos isn't just about stunning beaches; it's also a haven for delicious food and romantic settings. To make your special trip even more memorable, here are some of the best restaurants for couples on the island:

For the Intimate Ambiance:

- **Marmita:** Nestled in a charming garden setting, Marmita offers a magical atmosphere with twinkling lights and delicious Greek cuisine with a twist. Their upscale take on local ingredients creates a truly special dining experience.
- **Giardino Segreto Skiathos:** This hidden gem, translating to "Secret Garden," lives up to its name. Secluded and romantic, it boasts a beautiful courtyard setting and an enticing menu of Mediterranean dishes.
- **Siferi:** Located in the heart of Skiathos Town, Siferi offers a cozy and intimate atmosphere. The focus here is on fresh, seasonal seafood, perfect for a romantic candlelit dinner.

For Breathtaking Views:

- **The Windmill Restaurant:** Perched atop a hill, the Windmill Restaurant offers panoramic views of the Aegean Sea and nearby islands. Enjoy international and Greek specialties while taking in the

breathtaking scenery, perfect for a sunset dinner.
- **Agnadio:** This beachfront restaurant boasts stunning views of the water and serves up delectable Mediterranean cuisine. Watch the waves lap at the shore as you indulge in a delicious meal with your loved one.
- **Exantas Bar Restaurant:** Offering stunning sea views and a relaxed atmosphere, Exantas is a great choice for a romantic evening. Enjoy fresh seafood dishes and a wide selection of wines while taking in the beauty of Skiathos.

For a Special Occasion:

- **Black Pepper Restaurant:** Located within the Avalon Hotel, Black Pepper offers a luxurious setting and a menu featuring a fusion of Mediterranean and traditional Greek flavors. The ambiance is perfect for a celebratory dinner or a special occasion.
- **1901:** This elegant restaurant boasts a sophisticated atmosphere and a creative menu. Indulge in modern Greek cuisine with a focus on fresh, local ingredients for an unforgettable dining experience.
- **Crazy Cow Wine Bar Restaurant:** This lively restaurant offers a vibrant atmosphere

and a delicious menu. Enjoy an extensive wine list and a creative selection of dishes, perfect for a fun and memorable evening.

Remember:

- Consider making reservations in advance, especially for popular restaurants during peak season.
- If you have any dietary restrictions, be sure to let the restaurant know beforehand.
- Most importantly, relax, enjoy the delicious food, and savor the romantic atmosphere that Skiathos has to offer!

7.3. Family-Friendly Dining

Skiathos isn't just a haven for couples and romantic getaways; it's a fantastic destination for families as well! With its relaxed atmosphere, abundance of fresh seafood, and delicious Greek cuisine, Skiathos offers a variety of dining options that cater to all palates, including even the pickiest eaters. Here are some family-friendly restaurants you can explore:

Taverna Treats:

- **Greek tavernas:** These are a must-try in Skiathos. Most tavernas offer outdoor seating, perfect for enjoying a relaxed meal with scenic views. Look for tavernas with playgrounds or ample space for children to roam around.Popular choices include **Taverna Maistrali** and **Green Park**, known for their friendly staff, delicious grilled meats,and fresh seafood options.
- **Pizzerias:** Kids love pizza, and Skiathos has them covered! Pizzerias like **Maria's Pizza** and **Jimmy's** offer a casual ambiance and a variety of pizzas with both classic and creative toppings.

Beachside Bites:

- **Beach tavernas:** Many beaches in Skiathos have tavernas right on the sand. These offer a scenic dining experience with the convenience of being close to the water. Kids can play in the sand while parents enjoy a leisurely meal.Popular options include **The Windmill** on Trullas beach and **Beach House Restaurant** on Vassiliki beach.

Kid-Friendly Considerations:

- **Menus:** Look for restaurants with children's menus offering familiar options like pasta dishes, chicken nuggets, and simple grilled meats.
- **Atmosphere:** Opt for places with a relaxed ambiance and outdoor seating where children can have some space to move around.
- **Amenities:** Some restaurants offer highchairs, booster seats, or even small playgrounds, making the dining experience even smoother.

Sweet Endings:

- **Gelato shops:** No family vacation is complete without gelato! Skiathos has numerous gelato shops serving up delicious and refreshing flavors.
- **Creperies:** Crepes are a popular dessert option in Greece, offering both sweet and savory varieties. They're a fun and delicious way to end a meal.

Tips:

- Consider reserving a table in advance, especially during peak season.

- Many restaurants offer lunch and dinner buffets, a great option for families with diverse appetites.
- Pack some small toys or games to keep younger children entertained while waiting for food.

By keeping these tips in mind, you can ensure that mealtimes in Skiathos are a fun and enjoyable experience for the whole family!

7.4. Budget-Friendly Eats

Skiathos isn't just about stunning beaches; it's also about indulging in delicious Greek cuisine. The good news? You can enjoy amazing food without blowing your travel budget. Here's how to eat well on Skiathos without breaking the bank:

Embrace Greek Street Food:

- **Gyros:** Succulent meat (chicken, pork, or lamb) wrapped in warm pita bread with onions, tomatoes, tzatziki sauce,and fries. They're incredibly affordable and perfect for a quick and satisfying lunch.

- **Souvlaki:** Skewers of marinated meat (chicken, pork, or lamb) grilled to perfection. Grab some fresh pita bread, top it with chopped tomatoes, onions, and tzatziki for a delicious and budget-friendly meal.
- **Crepes & Souvlaki Lafka:** These street food stalls offer a variety of sweet and savory crepes, as well as "laffa" wraps filled with meat, vegetables, and sauces. Perfect for a grab-and-go meal or a late-night snack.

Local Tavernas:

- **Meze:** Sample a variety of small plates like dolmades (stuffed grape leaves), fried courgettes, tzatziki, grilled halloumi cheese, and fresh salads. Sharing a meze amongst friends is a delicious and social way to experience Greek cuisine.
- **Lunch Specials:** Many tavernas offer midday specials with lower prices than the dinner menu. Look out for these deals to enjoy a full meal at a fraction of the cost.
- **Family-run tavernas:** Often located outside the main tourist areas, these tavernas offer a more authentic experience with lower prices.

Self-Catering:

- **Stock Up at the Supermarket:** Pick up fresh fruits, vegetables, bread, cheese, and Greek yogurt for picnics on the beach or light meals at your accommodation.
- **Bakery Delights:** Local bakeries offer delicious pastries, breads, and sandwiches perfect for breakfast or a light lunch.

Insider Tips:

- Head to tavernas located away from the main harbor area for potentially lower prices.
- Look for tavernas with daily fresh fish specials, often priced by weight.
- Enjoy happy hour deals on drinks and snacks at some restaurants and bars.
- Opt for water or local wine instead of imported drinks to keep your bill down.
- Consider grabbing a delicious and filling souvlaki for lunch and a lighter dinner to save some euros.

By following these tips, you can savor the incredible flavors of Skiathos without emptying your wallet. So, grab a seat at a local taverna, order a meze, and get ready for a delicious and affordable Greek adventure!

7.5. Local Markets and Street Food

Skiathos isn't just about stunning beaches; it's also a haven for foodies. Alongside the delicious tavernas, the island offers a vibrant market scene and a treasure trove of tempting street food.

Local Markets:

- **Skiathos Town Market:** Nestled in the heart of the old town, this bustling market overflows with fresh, local produce. Find seasonal fruits and vegetables, plump olives, glistening fish, and fragrant herbs. Don't miss the opportunity to pick up some local honey or cheese for a taste of Skiathos at home.
- **Street Vendors:** Throughout the island, particularly in tourist areas, you'll find vendors selling beautiful handmade crafts and souvenirs. From colorful ceramics and woven goods to local jewelry and artwork, these little stalls are a great place to find unique gifts and a piece of Skiathos to take back with you.

Street Food Delights:

- **Gyros:** A quintessential Greek street food, gyros are marinated meat (usually chicken, pork, or lamb) cooked on a vertical rotisserie and served in warm pita bread with onions, tomatoes, tzatziki sauce, and french fries.
- **Souvlaki:** Similar to gyros, souvlaki features skewered meat (usually pork or chicken) grilled to perfection and served in a pita with similar toppings.
- **Loukoumades:** These melt-in-your-mouth Greek donuts are a must-try. Fried golden brown and drizzled with honey, cinnamon, or chocolate sauce, they're a delicious treat enjoyed hot or cold.
- **Meze:** For a taste of Skiathos' culinary tapestry, try meze. This selection of small plates features various local specialties like fried vegetables, dolmades (stuffed vine leaves), dips like hummus and fava, cheese saganaki, and fresh seafood.

Tips:

- Street food vendors typically operate during the day and early evening.
- Look for stalls with a steady stream of customers, often a good indicator of fresh and delicious food.

- Cash is usually preferred at street vendors, so come prepared.
- Don't be afraid to try something new! Embrace the flavors and enjoy the authentic Skiathos experience.

By exploring the local markets and indulging in street food, you'll gain a deeper appreciation for Skiathos' culinary scene and vibrant culture.

Chapter 8. Shopping

8.1. Local Markets and Souvenirs

Skiathos isn't just about stunning beaches; it also boasts a vibrant shopping scene. From traditional treasures to unique finds, here's your guide to Skiathos' local markets and souvenirs:

Treasure Hunting in Local Markets:

- **Weekly Farmer's Market:** Immerse yourself in the sights and smells of fresh produce at the weekly farmer's market. Stock up on juicy melons, plump tomatoes, hand-picked olives, and local honey – perfect for creating delicious meals in your villa or apartment.
- **The Old Port:** Stroll along the charming Old Port and browse stalls overflowing with handcrafted goods. Find unique pottery adorned with intricate designs, woven baskets perfect for beach picnics, and colorful textiles ideal for home décor.
- **Papadiamantis Street:** This bustling pedestrian street in Skiathos Town is a shopper's paradise. Find a treasure trove of souvenirs alongside local shops selling clothing, jewelry, and leather goods. Be sure

to keep an eye out for handmade sandals, a quintessential Greek summer staple.

Unforgettable Skiathos Souvenirs:

- **Embroidered Goods:** Take home a piece of Skiathos tradition with beautifully embroidered tablecloths, napkins, or even pillowcases. Look for intricate patterns depicting flowers, seashells, or mythological creatures.
- **Handmade Ceramics:** Skiathos boasts a rich pottery tradition. Find stunning vases, plates, and decorative items with vibrant colors and unique designs, perfect for adding a touch of Greece to your home.
- **Local Honey:** Drizzled on fresh bread or enjoyed on its own, Skiathos honey is a delicious and healthy souvenir. Look for varieties infused with local citrus flavors like orange or lemon for an extra twist.
- **Olive Oil:** Greece is renowned for its olive oil, and Skiathos is no exception. Bring back a bottle (or two!) of extra virgin olive oil, perfect for drizzling on salads, vegetables, or even enjoying with crusty bread.
- **Evil Eye Charm (Mat چشم نظر):** A popular souvenir throughout Greece, the evil eye charm is believed to ward off negativity. Find

these colorful glass trinkets in various shapes and sizes, a unique way to remember your Skiathos adventure.

Insider Tips:

- **Haggling is expected:** Don't be afraid to politely bargain, especially at smaller shops and open-air markets. It's all part of the local shopping experience!
- **Support local artisans:** Look for shops with handmade goods created by local craftspeople. You're not only taking home a unique souvenir but also supporting the island's creative community.
- **Shop early for the best selection:** Popular items can sell out quickly, especially during peak season. Head to the shops in the mornings for the freshest produce and widest variety of souvenirs.
- **Bring a reusable shopping bag:** Help reduce plastic waste by bringing your own reusable bag when shopping at the market or local stores.

By exploring Skiathos' local markets and bringing home a piece of the island's charm, you'll extend your vacation memories long after you return home.

8.2. Boutiques and Artisan Shops

Beyond the idyllic beaches and vibrant nightlife, Skiathos boasts a treasure trove of unique shops waiting to be explored.From trendy boutiques to charming artisan stores, here's your guide to indulging in some retail therapy:

Boutique Bonanza:

- **Papadiamantis Street:** This bustling heart of Skiathos Town is lined with an array of boutiques catering to all styles. Discover trendy beachwear, statement jewelry, and stylish clothing perfect for island evenings.
- **Skiathos Marina:** For the fashionistas, the marina area offers a touch of luxury with several high-end designer boutiques showcasing the latest collections.
- **Ammos by Kitty (Laskou 6):** This charming boutique is a haven for beach lovers. Find handcrafted sandals,unique jewelry pieces, and stylish accessories to complete your island look.
- **Theros Skiathos Boutique (Skiathos Town):** This highly-rated boutique offers a curated selection of clothing,shoes, and

accessories, all with a focus on quality and style.

Artisan Delights:

- **Archipelago (near Papadiamandis House):** A treasure trove for lovers of Greek art and folklore. This world-class store showcases exquisite textiles, handcrafted jewelry, and sculptures that reflect the island's rich heritage.
- **Galerie Varsakis (Trion Ierarchon Square):** Step into a museum-like setting and explore a collection of folk antiques, embroidered linens, and unique rugs from around the world.
- **Gallery Seraina (Papadiamandis Street):** For a touch of whimsy, browse through Gallery Seraina's collection of ceramic plates, handcrafted jewelry, and unique glasswork.
- **Local Artisanal Markets:** Scattered throughout the island, discover local markets where artisans showcase their creations. Find traditional pottery, woven goods, handmade soaps, and local honey, all perfect mementos of your Skiathos adventure.

Tips for Shopping Success:

- **Haggling is acceptable:** In some smaller shops and local markets, friendly haggling is part of the shopping experience.
- **Look for local crafts:** Support the local artisans by taking home a piece of Skiathos' artistic heritage.
- **Shop hours:** Most shops adhere to typical Greek opening hours, with a siesta break in the afternoon and extended hours during peak season.
- **Bring cash:** While many stores accept cards, some smaller shops may prefer cash transactions.

Embrace the spirit of discovery and get ready to find unique treasures that capture the essence of Skiathos!

8.3. Shopping Tips and Etiquette

Skiathos boasts a treasure trove of shopping delights, from traditional handicrafts to designer boutiques. Here are some tips and etiquette pointers to navigate the island's shopping scene like a pro:

Local Charm:

- **The Heart of the Action:** Skiathos Town (Chora) is the main shopping hub. Explore the labyrinthine streets lined with shops selling everything from ceramics and jewelry to clothing and local delicacies.
- **Treasure Hunt:** Venture outside Chora and discover unique finds in smaller villages like Tzaneria, known for its leather goods, and Kastro, where you might find hidden gems in local stores.

Bargaining with Grace:

- **Haggling Accepted:** In smaller, independent shops, bargaining is an acceptable practice. It's a cultural dance – be polite, respectful, and start with a reasonable offer.
- **Set Your Limits:** Know your budget and be prepared to walk away if you don't reach an agreement.
- **Respect the Craft:** Remember, handmade items take time and skill. Don't be lowballing – fair offers are appreciated.

Shopping Savvy:

- **Keep an Eye Out for Sales:** Sales are common during the off-season (around

October and May). You might score amazing deals on clothes, jewelry, and souvenirs.
- **Receipt, Please:** Always ask for a receipt, especially for high-value items. It's helpful in case of exchanges or returns.
- **Support Local Artisans:** Look out for locally-made products like ceramics, embroidery, and leather goods. These treasures make excellent souvenirs and support the island's artisans.

Eco-Conscious Shopping:

- **Think Reusable:** Opt for reusable bags instead of plastic ones. Many shops offer beautiful woven tote bags that are perfect for your purchases.
- **Mindful Materials:** If you're buying clothes or souvenirs, consider natural materials like cotton or linen. They're better for the environment and cooler in summer weather.

Remember:

- **Embrace the Experience:** Shopping in Skiathos is a cultural experience. Enjoy the interaction with friendly shopkeepers and soak up the atmosphere.

- **Shop with a Smile:** A friendly smile goes a long way. You'll receive much better service with a positive attitude.
- **Happy Shopping!:** With these tips in mind, you're all set to have a rewarding shopping adventure in Skiathos!

Chapter 9. Itineraries

9.1. Weekend Getaway

Day 1: Embrace the Beach Bum

- **Morning:** Arrive in Skiathos and check into your hotel. Leave your luggage and head straight to the nearest beach!Kick off your shoes, sink your toes in the sand, and soak up the Aegean sunshine. **Elias Beach** or **Megalos Amos**are great choices for turquoise waters and soft sand.
- **Afternoon:** After a relaxing morning, explore the charming town of Skiathos. Wander the narrow streets lined with whitewashed houses, colorful shops, and traditional tavernas. Don't forget to pick up some fresh, local produce from the market for a picnic lunch. In the afternoon heat, visit the **Folklore Museum** to delve into the island's history and culture.
- **Evening:** As the sun sets, take a boat tour from the old harbor to admire the dramatic coastline from the water.Look out for secluded coves and hidden beaches, and maybe even spot some dolphins along the way. Enjoy a delicious seafood dinner at a

waterfront taverna in the bustling port, watching the twinkling lights come alive.

Day 2: Island Adventures Await

- **Morning:** Rent a car or scooter and embark on an island adventure. Head north to **Kastro**, the medieval castle ruins offering panoramic views of the island. Explore the charming villages of **Kalivia** and **Καναλατα** (Kanaplata) with their traditional architecture and friendly locals. Stop for a refreshing swim at **Small Banana Beach** or **Lalaria Beach**, famous for its unique rock formations.
- **Afternoon:** In the afternoon, head to the southwestern part of the island to visit the beautiful **Monastery of Evangelistria**. Take in the serene atmosphere and admire the stunning views from the monastery's terrace.Afterward, cool off with a swim at **Koukounaries Beach**, a paradise with golden sand and crystal-clear waters.
- **Evening:** Enjoy a final night of fun in Skiathos town. Stroll along the lively harbor front, browse through the souvenir shops, and people-watch at the cafes. Savor a traditional Greek meal at a taverna with live music, soaking in the vibrant atmosphere.

Bonus:

- If you have extra time, consider taking a boat trip to one of the nearby islands, such as **Skopelos** or **Alonissos**, to discover their unique charm.

Tips:

- Pre-book car or scooter rentals, especially during peak season.
- Many beaches have sunbeds and umbrellas available for rent.
- Pack comfortable shoes for exploring the island's villages and historical sites.
- Don't forget to try some local specialties like **lobster spaghetti** and **almond pie**.

This itinerary provides a taste of what Skiathos has to offer. Feel free to adjust it based on your interests and preferences.Remember, the beauty of Skiathos lies in its relaxed pace, so be sure to slow down, savor the moment, and create unforgettable memories!

9.2. 5-Day Itinerary

Skiathos offers a perfect blend of relaxation, adventure, and cultural exploration. Here's a suggested 5-day itinerary to help you make the most of your time on this enchanting island:

Day 1: Arrival and Beach Bliss

- **Morning:** Arrive in Skiathos and check into your accommodation. Enjoy a leisurely lunch overlooking the picturesque harbor.
- **Afternoon:** Head to Koukounaries Beach, the island's most famous, for swimming, sunbathing, and water sports.
- **Evening:** Stroll through Skiathos Town, exploring its charming streets, boutique shops, and vibrant nightlife. Enjoy dinner at a waterfront taverna.

Day 2: Island Hopping and Beach Exploration

- **Morning:** Embark on a boat trip to the nearby islands of Tsougria and Alonissos. Explore hidden coves, snorkel in crystal-clear waters, and enjoy a delicious lunch on board.

- **Afternoon:** Return to Skiathos and relax on the secluded Elia Beach, known for its stunning natural beauty.
- **Evening:** Enjoy a romantic dinner at a beachfront restaurant, savoring fresh seafood and breathtaking sunsets.

Day 3: Cultural Exploration and Relaxation

- **Morning:** Visit the historic Kastro, Skiathos' Venetian castle, offering panoramic views of the town and harbor. Explore the charming narrow streets and admire the traditional architecture.
- **Afternoon:** Relax by the pool or indulge in a spa treatment. Alternatively, rent a bike and explore the island's countryside.
- **Evening:** Enjoy a traditional Greek night with live music, dancing, and delicious food at a local taverna.

Day 4: Adventure and Beach Hopping

- **Morning:** Go hiking in the lush green hills surrounding Skiathos Town. Enjoy stunning views and discover hidden trails.
- **Afternoon:** Visit Lalaria Beach, one of Greece's most iconic beaches, accessible only

by boat. Marvel at the white pebble beach and the crystal-clear turquoise waters.
- **Evening:** Enjoy a cocktail at a trendy beach bar and watch the sunset.

Day 5: Farewell to Skiathos

- **Morning:** Spend your last morning relaxing on your favorite beach or exploring the local markets for souvenirs.
- **Afternoon:** Enjoy a farewell lunch at a waterfront restaurant, savoring the flavors of Skiathos one last time.
- **Evening:** Depart for the airport, cherishing the memories of your unforgettable stay on Skiathos.

Note: This itinerary is just a suggestion. Feel free to customize it based on your interests and preferences. Skiathos offers a variety of activities and experiences, so explore and discover your own hidden gems!

9.3. 7-Day Itinerary

Day 1: Arrival and Relaxation

- Arrive in Skiathos and check into your accommodation.
- Enjoy a leisurely lunch at a waterfront taverna.
- Spend the afternoon relaxing on the beach, exploring the charming town of Skiathos, or taking a boat trip around the island to get a feel for its beauty.
- Enjoy a delicious dinner at a local restaurant, sampling traditional Greek cuisine.

Day 2: Beach Hopping and Water Sports

- Start your day with a hearty Greek breakfast.
- Head to Koukounaries Beach, one of the island's most famous beaches, with its golden sands and crystal-clear waters.
- Enjoy water sports like paddleboarding, kayaking, or jet skiing.
- Visit the nearby Banana Beach for a more secluded atmosphere.
- End the day with a cocktail at a beach bar and watch the sunset.

Day 3: Island Exploration and History

- Take a boat trip to the uninhabited island of Lalaria, famous for its unique rock formations and turquoise waters.

- Explore the picturesque village of Kastro, the old capital of Skiathos, perched on a hilltop with stunning views.
- Visit the Monastery of Evangelistria, a significant religious site with a rich history.
- Enjoy a traditional Greek dinner in Kastro.

Day 4: Sailing and Island Hopping

- Embark on a day-sailing trip to the neighboring islands of Skopelos and Alonissos.
- Explore the charming town of Skopelos, known for its beautiful harbor and lush greenery.
- Visit Kastani Beach, made famous by the movie "Mamma Mia!".
- Relax on the boat and enjoy the stunning scenery.

Day 5: Relaxation and Indulgence

- Spend a lazy day by the pool or beach, soaking up the sun.
- Indulge in a spa treatment to relax and rejuvenate.
- Enjoy a romantic dinner at a waterfront restaurant.

Day 6: Adventure and Nature

- Hike to the top of Mount Enos for breathtaking panoramic views of the island.
- Visit the Asselinos Cave, a natural wonder with stunning stalactites and stalagmites.
- Enjoy a picnic lunch in the shade of the pine trees.

Day 7: Farewell to Skiathos

- Spend your last morning relaxing on your favorite beach or exploring the local markets for souvenirs.
- Enjoy a farewell lunch at a traditional taverna.
- Head to the airport with unforgettable memories of your Skiathos adventure.

Note: This itinerary is just a suggestion, and you can customize it based on your interests and preferences. Skiathos offers a variety of activities and experiences, so don't hesitate to explore beyond this plan.

9.4. Itinerary for Solo Travelers

Skiathos is a fantastic destination for solo travelers, offering a perfect blend of relaxation, adventure, and opportunities to meet fellow explorers. Here's a suggested itinerary to help you make the most of your solo adventure:

Days 1-2: Relax and Explore Skiathos Town

- **Day 1:** Arrive in Skiathos and settle into your accommodation. Spend the afternoon exploring the charming streets of Skiathos Town, soaking up the vibrant atmosphere. Enjoy a leisurely dinner at a seaside taverna, watching the sunset over the harbor.
- **Day 2:** Rent a scooter or bike to explore the island's coastline. Visit the picturesque Kastro, the island's historic Venetian castle, offering stunning panoramic views. Spend the afternoon relaxing on one of the nearby beaches,such as Megali Ammos or Koukounaries.

Days 3-4: Island Hopping and Beach Bliss

- **Day 3:** Embark on a boat trip to the nearby islands of Skopelos and Alonissos. Explore

the charming villages,pristine beaches, and lush landscapes.
- **Day 4:** Spend a day indulging in the island's beach life. Choose from a variety of secluded coves or lively beach bars. Consider joining a beach club for a day of pampering and socializing.

Days 5-6: Adventure and Relaxation

- **Day 5:** Rent a kayak or paddleboard and explore the island's coastline from a different perspective. Discover hidden coves and enjoy the tranquility of the sea.
- **Day 6:** Take a day trip to Lalaria Beach, one of Skiathos' most iconic landmarks. This stunning beach, accessible only by boat, is a must-visit for any traveler.

Day 7: Farewell to Skiathos

- Enjoy a leisurely breakfast and soak up the island vibes one last time. Perhaps visit a local market for souvenirs or indulge in a final delicious Greek meal before departing.

Additional Tips:

- Don't be afraid to strike up conversations with fellow travelers. Many people are open to making new friends.
- Join group activities or excursions to meet like-minded individuals.
- Embrace the solo experience and enjoy your own company.
- Take advantage of the island's nightlife, with its lively bars and clubs.

Remember: This is just a suggested itinerary, and you should feel free to customize it based on your interests and preferences. Skiathos offers a wealth of experiences, so explore, relax, and create your own unforgettable solo adventure.

9.5. Itinerary for Families

Skiathos is a fantastic destination for families, offering a perfect blend of relaxation, adventure, and fun for all ages. Here's a suggested itinerary to help you plan your family vacation:

Day 1: Arrival and Beach Bliss

- **Morning:** Arrive at Skiathos Airport and transfer to your accommodation.

- **Afternoon:** Head to Koukounaries Beach, a family-friendly paradise with shallow waters, water sports, and beachside tavernas. Relax, build sandcastles, and enjoy the crystal-clear waters.
- **Evening:** Enjoy a delicious family dinner at a taverna overlooking the sea.

Day 2: Exploring the Island and Waterpark Fun

- **Morning:** Take a boat trip around the island, stopping at secluded coves and beaches like Lalaria Beach. Many boat trips offer snorkeling and swimming opportunities.
- **Afternoon:** Visit the Skiathos Waterpark for a day of thrilling slides, lazy rivers, and splash pads.
- **Evening:** Treat the family to ice cream or a refreshing drink at one of Skiathos Town's charming cafes.

Day 3: Pirate Adventure and Relaxation

- **Morning:** Embark on a pirate-themed boat trip, complete with treasure hunts, water games, and a delicious lunch.

- **Afternoon:** Visit Kastro, the old town of Skiathos, with its charming narrow streets, Venetian castle, and stunning views.
- **Evening:** Enjoy a family-friendly dinner at a taverna with traditional Greek music and dancing.

Day 4: Beach Hopping and Farewell

- **Morning:** Spend the morning relaxing on a different beach, perhaps Agia Eleni Beach, known for its calm waters and lush surroundings.
- **Afternoon:** Enjoy some last-minute shopping for souvenirs or local delicacies.
- **Evening:** Share a farewell dinner with your family, reminiscing about your unforgettable Skiathos adventure.

Additional Tips:

- Pack plenty of sunscreen, hats, and sunglasses for everyone.
- Bring comfortable walking shoes for exploring the island.
- Consider renting a car or scooter for added flexibility (if age-appropriate).

- Don't miss the opportunity to try delicious Greek cuisine, including souvlaki, moussaka, and fresh seafood.
- Take advantage of the island's rich history and culture by visiting local museums and historical sites.

This itinerary offers a balance of relaxation, adventure, and cultural experiences, making it perfect for families with children of all ages. Remember to adapt the itinerary based on your family's interests and preferences.

9.6. Romantic Getaway for Couples

Skiathos, with its enchanting coves, picturesque villages, and vibrant sunsets, is a perfect backdrop for a romantic getaway. Here's a suggested itinerary to inspire your couple's adventure:

Day 1: Arrival and Relaxation

- **Afternoon:** Arrive in Skiathos and check into your chosen accommodation. Consider a boutique hotel with a private balcony or a luxurious villa with a plunge pool for ultimate privacy.

- **Evening:** Enjoy a leisurely stroll through the charming streets of Skiathos Town, exploring the shops, boutiques, and charming squares. Find a cozy taverna with a sea view for a romantic dinner.

Day 2: Beach Bliss and Island Exploration

- **Morning:** Start your day with a delicious breakfast at your hotel and then head to Koukounaries Beach, one of Skiathos' most famous beaches. Rent a sunbed and umbrella for a relaxing day in the sun.
- **Afternoon:** Take a boat trip to the secluded Lalaria Beach, known for its dramatic white cliffs and turquoise waters. Pack a picnic and enjoy a private moment on this stunning beach.
- **Evening:** Return to Skiathos Town for a romantic dinner at a waterfront restaurant, savoring fresh seafood and local delicacies.

Day 3: Monastery and Sunset Cruise

- **Morning:** Visit the Monastery of Evangelistria, a historic landmark with breathtaking views. Explore the monastery's serene gardens and learn about its rich history.

- **Afternoon:** Indulge in a couples' massage at a local spa to relax and rejuvenate.
- **Evening:** Embark on a sunset cruise, sipping champagne as you admire the golden hues of the sky. Many cruises offer romantic dinner options as well.

Day 4: Island Hopping and Beach Escape

- **Morning:** Rent a boat or join a boat tour to explore the nearby islands of Skopelos and Alonissos. These islands offer a more secluded and tranquil atmosphere.
- **Afternoon:** Return to Skiathos and spend a lazy afternoon at a secluded beach like Agia Eleni, known for its crystal-clear waters and peaceful ambiance.
- **Evening:** Enjoy a romantic dinner at a beachside taverna, with the sound of waves as your soundtrack.

Day 5: Farewell to Paradise

- **Morning:** Enjoy a leisurely breakfast and soak up the last moments of your romantic getaway. Perhaps take a final stroll through Skiathos Town to find unique souvenirs.

- **Afternoon:** Depart for the airport, carrying with you unforgettable memories of your time in Skiathos.

Tips for a Romantic Getaway:

- Choose accommodations with private balconies or terraces for intimate moments.
- Pack comfortable beachwear, elegant evening attire, and casual outfits for exploring the island.
- Surprise your partner with small gifts or romantic gestures throughout your trip.
- Don't forget to capture your special moments with plenty of photos.

Remember, this is just a suggestion, and you can customize the itinerary based on your preferences and interests. Enjoy your romantic escape to Skiathos!

Chapter 10. Traveling with Kids

10.1. Kid-Friendly Attractions

Skiathos isn't just a haven for adults; it's also a fantastic destination for families. With its pristine beaches, charming villages, and a laid-back atmosphere, it offers plenty of fun activities to keep the little ones entertained.

Beach Bliss for the Whole Family

Skiathos boasts a plethora of kid-friendly beaches with shallow, crystal-clear waters perfect for paddling and building sandcastles. Here are a few top picks:

- **Koukounaries Beach:** This long, sandy beach offers a gentle slope into the sea, making it ideal for families with young children. It also features a variety of water sports and beachside tavernas.
- **Troulos Beach:** Another family-friendly option, Troulos offers a mix of sand and pebbles, as well as a selection of water sports and beach bars.
- **Mandraki Beach:** This sheltered bay is perfect for swimming and snorkeling, with calm waters and a relaxed atmosphere.

Adventures for Young Explorers

Beyond the beaches, Skiathos offers a range of activities to keep kids entertained:

- **Boat Trips:** Embark on a family-friendly boat trip to explore hidden coves, swim in secluded bays, and spot dolphins.
- **Water Sports:** Many beaches offer a variety of water sports suitable for children, such as paddleboarding, kayaking, and banana boat rides.
- **Monastery of Panagia Evangelistria:** This historic monastery is a fascinating place to visit with kids. They can learn about the island's history and admire the beautiful architecture.
- **Skiathitiko Spiti:** This traditional Greek house museum offers a glimpse into island life, with interactive exhibits that will engage young minds.

Dining with the Little Ones

Skiathos boasts a variety of family-friendly restaurants offering delicious Greek cuisine and kid-friendly options. Many tavernas have outdoor seating areas with playgrounds or play areas, allowing parents to relax while the kids play.

Remember, Skiathos is all about slowing down and enjoying quality family time. With its beautiful beaches, friendly locals, and relaxed atmosphere, it's the perfect destination for a memorable family vacation.

10.2. Activities for Children

Skiathos is not just a paradise for adults; it's also a haven for families with children. With its pristine beaches, exciting water sports, and charming villages, there's something to keep every young adventurer entertained.

Beach Bliss

- **Sandy Playgrounds:** Many of Skiathos' beaches offer shallow, calm waters, perfect for building sandcastles, splashing around, and collecting seashells. Koukounaries and Troulos are particularly child-friendly.
- **Water Sports Fun:** Older kids will love trying out water sports like paddleboarding, kayaking, and snorkeling. There are plenty of rental shops offering equipment and lessons.

- **Boat Trips:** Family-friendly boat trips often include swimming stops at secluded coves, making for a memorable day out.

Island Adventures

- **Explore the Town:** Skiathos Town is a charming place to wander with kids. They'll love the colorful shops, ice cream parlors, and the chance to spot airplanes taking off and landing.
- **Visit Kastro:** The old town of Kastro offers a glimpse into Skiathos' history and stunning views. Kids will enjoy exploring the narrow streets and imagining life as a pirate.
- **Monkey Island:** A visit to Monkey Island is a fun excursion for the whole family. Kids can interact with the friendly primates in a safe environment.

Other Fun Activities

- **Water Parks:** While not on the island itself, there are water parks on nearby islands like Skiathos which offer a day of thrilling water slides and lazy rivers.
- **Kids' Clubs:** Some hotels and resorts offer kids' clubs with supervised activities, giving parents a chance to relax.

Remember to pack plenty of sunscreen, hats, and comfortable shoes for your little ones. With its laid-back atmosphere and family-friendly attractions, Skiathos is sure to create lasting memories for your children.

10.3. Tips for Parents

Skiathos isn't just a haven for couples and groups of friends; it's also a fantastic destination for families. With its pristine beaches, charming villages, and relaxed atmosphere, it offers the perfect backdrop for creating unforgettable family memories. Here are some tips to help you plan your family vacation to Skiathos:

Choosing the Right Accommodation

- **Family-Friendly Resorts:** Many hotels and resorts on Skiathos cater to families with amenities like kids' clubs, pools, and family-sized rooms.
- **Villas and Apartments:** For more privacy and space, consider renting a villa or apartment with a private pool or garden.

- **Location Matters:** Choose accommodation close to family-friendly beaches, restaurants, and activities.

Beach Bliss for the Whole Family

- **Safe Swimming:** Look for beaches with gradual slopes and lifeguards, especially if you have young children.
- **Water Sports:** Many beaches offer a range of water sports suitable for different ages, from paddleboarding and kayaking to banana boat rides.
- **Beach Clubs:** Some beach clubs provide children's entertainment and facilities, giving parents a chance to relax.

Family-Friendly Activities

- **Boat Trips:** Explore the surrounding islands and hidden coves on a family-friendly boat trip.
- **Pirate Cruises:** Kids will love the adventure of a pirate-themed boat trip with treasure hunts and water games.
- **Kastro:** Discover the island's history together while exploring the medieval Kastro.

- **Water Parks:** Although not on Skiathos, there are water parks on nearby islands that offer a fun-filled day out for the whole family.

Dining with Kids

- **Family-Friendly Taverns:** Many tavernas offer children's menus and highchairs.
- **Picnics:** Pack a picnic lunch for a relaxed day at the beach.
- **Ice Cream Parlors:** Treat the kids to a delicious ice cream after a day in the sun.

Tips for Traveling with Kids

- **Pack Essentials:** Don't forget essentials like sunscreen, hats, insect repellent, and a well-stocked first-aid kit.
- **Bring Favorite Toys:** Familiar toys can help keep kids entertained during travel and downtime.
- **Flexible Itinerary:** Be prepared to adjust your plans based on your children's needs and interests.

By following these tips, you can create a memorable family vacation to Skiathos that everyone will enjoy.

10.4. Family Accommodation Recommendations

Skiathos is a fantastic destination for families, offering a perfect blend of relaxation, adventure, and fun. Choosing the right accommodation is key to a memorable family vacation. Here are some options to consider:

Hotels and Resorts

For families seeking comfort and convenience, hotels and resorts are a great choice. Many offer a range of amenities perfect for kids, such as children's pools, playgrounds, and kids' clubs.

- **Skiathos Princess Resort:** This luxurious resort boasts spacious rooms, a water park, and a kids' club, making it a top choice for families.
- **Kassandra Bay Resort, Suites & Spa:** This family-friendly resort offers stunning sea views, multiple pools, and a kids' play area.

Apartments and Villas

For families who prefer more space and independence, apartments and villas are an excellent option. They often come with fully equipped kitchens, allowing you to prepare meals at your convenience.

- **Poseidon Villas:** These spacious villas offer privacy and stunning sea views, making them ideal for families.
- **Amalthia Studios:** These family-friendly apartments are located in a peaceful area, yet close to the beach and amenities.

Tips for Choosing Family Accommodation:

- **Location:** Consider the proximity to beaches, restaurants, and other family-friendly attractions.
- **Amenities:** Look for accommodations with children's pools, playgrounds, or kids' clubs.
- **Space:** Ensure the accommodation is spacious enough for your family.
- **Safety:** Prioritize safety features like balconies with safety rails and non-slip surfaces around pools.

Remember: Booking in advance is recommended, especially during peak season.

By carefully considering these factors, you can find the perfect family accommodation for your unforgettable Skiathos vacation.

Chapter 11. Traveling Solo

11.1. Safety Tips for Solo Travelers

Skiathos is generally a safe island for solo travelers. However, like any destination, it's essential to take precautions to ensure a worry-free trip. Here are some tips to keep you safe during your solo adventure:

General Safety Tips

- **Research:** Familiarize yourself with the island, its customs, and local laws before your trip.
- **Inform Loved Ones:** Share your itinerary with friends or family back home, including your accommodation details.
- **Travel Insurance:** It's essential to have comprehensive travel insurance that covers medical emergencies, lost luggage, and trip cancellations.
- **Trust Your Gut:** If something feels off, it probably is. Don't hesitate to trust your instincts.

Personal Safety

- **Valuables:** Avoid carrying large amounts of cash or displaying expensive jewelry.
- **Stay Aware:** Be mindful of your surroundings, especially in crowded areas.
- **Nighttime Precautions:** While Skiathos is generally safe, it's advisable to avoid isolated areas alone at night.
- **Transportation:** Use reputable taxis or public transportation. Verify the driver's license before entering a taxi.

Health and Safety

- **Sun Protection:** Protect yourself from the strong Greek sun with sunscreen, a hat, and sunglasses.
- **Hydration:** Stay hydrated by drinking plenty of water, especially during hot weather.
- **Food Hygiene:** Be cautious when choosing street food and ensure proper hygiene when dining out.
- **Medical Kit:** Pack a basic first-aid kit with essentials like band-aids, antiseptic, and any necessary medications.

Making Connections

- **Connect with Other Travelers:** Consider staying in hostels or guesthouses to meet fellow solo travelers.
- **Join Group Tours:** This is a great way to meet like-minded people and explore the island with a guide.
- **Local Interactions:** Engage with locals respectfully and learn a few basic Greek phrases.

By following these safety tips, you can enjoy your solo adventure in Skiathos to the fullest while minimizing potential risks. Remember, common sense and awareness are your best allies.

11.2. Best Places to Meet People

Skiathos is not just a stunning island; it's a social hub brimming with opportunities to connect with fellow travelers and locals alike. Here are some of the best spots to mingle and make new friends:

Beach Bars and Clubs

- **Koukounaries Beach:** This iconic beach is a magnet for young and lively crowds. The beach bars offer a perfect setting to relax, enjoy refreshing drinks, and strike up conversations with fellow sun-seekers.

- **Banana Beach:** Known for its laid-back atmosphere and vibrant music scene, Banana Beach is a great place to meet people from all walks of life.
- **Paradise Beach:** With its lively party scene, Paradise Beach is ideal for those seeking a more energetic social environment.

Taverns and Restaurants

- **Old Town:** The charming alleys of Skiathos Town are lined with traditional tavernas where locals and tourists gather to enjoy delicious food and good company.
- **Harborfront Restaurants:** Enjoy a meal with a view while mingling with other diners at one of the many harborfront restaurants.

Bars and Clubs

- **Bar Street:** This lively strip is the heart of Skiathos' nightlife, offering a wide variety of bars, clubs, and live music venues.
- **Old Town Bars:** Discover hidden gems in the winding streets of the Old Town, where you can enjoy a more intimate atmosphere and connect with locals.

Boat Trips and Excursions

- **Island Hopping Cruises:** Join a boat trip to explore neighboring islands and meet fellow travelers on board.
- **Boat Parties:** For a more lively experience, consider a boat party where you can dance, drink, and socialize with other partygoers.

Water Sports and Activities

- **Beach Volleyball:** Join a game of beach volleyball to meet other active and sociable people.
- **Watersports Centers:** Participate in water sports activities like paddleboarding or kayaking to connect with fellow adventurers.

Tips for Meeting People

- **Be Open and Approachable:** Smile, initiate conversations, and show genuine interest in others.
- **Join Group Activities:** Participate in organized tours, excursions, or group events to meet like-minded people.
- **Leverage Social Media:** Use travel-related social media platforms and apps to connect with other travelers before and during your trip.

- **Embrace the Local Culture:** Immerse yourself in local customs and traditions to connect with locals and other travelers interested in cultural experiences.

Remember, Skiathos is a friendly island where it's easy to make new connections. With a little effort and an open mind, you're sure to create lasting memories and friendships.

11.3. Solo Activities and Experiences

Skiathos is a fantastic destination for solo travelers, offering a perfect blend of relaxation and exploration. Here are some ideas to inspire your solo adventure:

Beach Bliss and Solitude

- **Beach Hopping:** With over 60 beaches to choose from, Skiathos is a beach lover's paradise. Pack a good book, your favorite tunes, and embark on a beach-hopping adventure.
- **Water Sports:** Indulge in thrilling water sports like windsurfing, paddleboarding, or kayaking. Many water sports centers offer

lessons for beginners, making it easy to try something new.
- **Sunset Soaking:** Find a secluded spot on the beach and watch the sun paint the sky in vibrant colors. It's a truly magical experience.

Exploring the Island Alone

- **Hiking Adventures:** Escape the crowds and immerse yourself in nature by hiking through the island's lush greenery. The trails offer stunning views and a chance to connect with the island's natural beauty.
- **Cultural Discoveries:** Visit historical sites like Kastro, the medieval castle, or explore charming villages like Kastro and Klima. Immerse yourself in the island's rich history and culture.
- **Boat Trips:** Rent a boat or join a boat tour to explore hidden coves and beaches. Enjoy the freedom of the open sea and discover secluded spots away from the crowds.

Relax and Recharge

- **Spa Day:** Treat yourself to a relaxing spa day and pamper yourself with massages, facials, or other wellness treatments.

- **Bookworm's Haven:** Find a cozy café or beachfront taverna with a good book and enjoy some peaceful reading time.
- **People Watching:** Grab a seat at a lively taverna and enjoy people-watching while savoring delicious Greek cuisine.

Connecting with Other Travelers

While solo travel offers incredible freedom, it's also a great opportunity to meet like-minded people.

- **Join Group Tours:** Consider joining group tours or activities to meet fellow travelers.
- **Socialize at Beach Clubs:** Many beach clubs offer a lively atmosphere where you can easily strike up conversations.
- **Utilize Social Media:** Join travel groups or forums to connect with other solo travelers before or during your trip.

Remember, Skiathos is a friendly island where locals are welcoming to visitors. Don't hesitate to strike up conversations with locals or other travelers. Embrace the adventure and create unforgettable memories on your solo journey!

11.4. Budget-Friendly Tips

Skiathos doesn't have to break the bank, especially for solo adventurers! Here are some tips to help you enjoy your trip without draining your wallet:

Accommodation

- **Hostels and Guesthouses:** Opt for budget-friendly accommodations like hostels or guesthouses. These often offer shared facilities but can save you a significant amount.
- **Apartment Rentals:** Consider renting a studio apartment for a more independent and potentially cheaper option.
- **Camping:** If you're adventurous, camping can be a very affordable way to experience Skiathos. Check for designated camping areas or explore the possibility of wild camping (always check local regulations).

Transportation

- **Walking:** Skiathos is relatively small, and many attractions are within walking distance. Embrace the opportunity to explore on foot and save on transportation costs.

- **Public Buses:** Utilize the local bus system to get around the island. It's a budget-friendly way to reach different beaches and villages.
- **Bike Rentals:** Renting a bike can be a fun and affordable way to explore the island at your own pace.

Food and Drink

- **Local Tavernas:** Enjoy authentic Greek cuisine at local tavernas. These often offer more affordable options than touristy restaurants.
- **Market Fresh:** Buy fresh produce, bread, and cheese from local markets for delicious and budget-friendly picnics.
- **Meze Sharing:** Order a variety of meze dishes to share with other solo travelers or enjoy a delicious meal on your own.
- **Happy Hour:** Take advantage of happy hour deals at bars and restaurants to save on drinks.

Activities

- **Free Beaches:** Skiathos boasts numerous free public beaches, so you don't have to spend money to enjoy the sun and sea.

- **Hiking and Nature:** Explore the island's natural beauty through hiking trails. This is a free activity that offers stunning views.
- **Free Walking Tours:** Many towns offer free walking tours, providing a great way to learn about the local history and culture.
- **Join Group Activities:** Consider joining group tours or activities to share costs and meet fellow travelers.

Additional Tips

- **Cook Your Own Meals:** Having a kitchen in your accommodation allows you to prepare your own meals, saving money on dining out.
- **Off-Peak Travel:** Consider visiting Skiathos during the shoulder seasons (spring or autumn) for potentially lower prices on flights, accommodation, and activities.
- **Use Free Wi-Fi:** Take advantage of free Wi-Fi at cafes, restaurants, and accommodations to stay connected without incurring data charges.

By following these tips, you can enjoy an unforgettable solo adventure in Skiathos without breaking the bank.

Chapter 12. Romantic Getaways

12.1. *Romantic Activities and Spots*

Skiathos, with its enchanting blend of sun-kissed beaches, charming villages, and vibrant sunsets, is a perfect backdrop for a romantic getaway. Here are some ideas to inspire your couple's retreat:

Romantic Activities

- **Sunset Cruises:** Sail into the horizon as the sun paints the sky in hues of pink and orange. Enjoy champagne, canapés, and each other's company on a private yacht or a shared catamaran.
- **Beach Picnics:** Pack a basket filled with delicious treats and head to a secluded beach. Enjoy a romantic picnic under the shade of an umbrella, with the gentle lapping of waves as your soundtrack.
- **Spa Day:** Indulge in a couples' massage or a pampering spa treatment together. Relax and rejuvenate in a serene environment, leaving you feeling refreshed and connected.
- **Romantic Dinner:** Book a table at a waterfront restaurant with stunning views. Enjoy a candlelit dinner featuring fresh

seafood and local delicacies, accompanied by a bottle of fine wine.
- **Stargazing:** Escape the city lights and find a secluded spot to stargaze. Lie side by side, marveling at the celestial wonders above.

Romantic Spots

- **Lalaria Beach:** This iconic beach, with its white pebbles and crystal-clear waters, is a perfect spot for a romantic swim or a leisurely stroll hand-in-hand.
- **Kastro:** Explore the ruins of the Venetian castle, offering panoramic views of the town and the sea. Share a kiss as the sun sets over the horizon.
- **Koubourou Beach:** This secluded cove with its turquoise waters and lush greenery is an ideal spot for a private and intimate moment.
- **Agia Eleni Beach:** Known for its romantic atmosphere, this beach offers a charming setting for a leisurely day together.

Whether you're seeking adventure, relaxation, or simply quality time together, Skiathos offers an abundance of romantic experiences. Let the island's magic cast a spell on you and create unforgettable memories with your loved one.

12.2. Couple's Itinerary

Skiathos, with its enchanting blend of sun-kissed beaches, charming villages, and vibrant nightlife, is the perfect backdrop for a romantic getaway. Here's a suggested itinerary for couples seeking to create unforgettable memories on this idyllic Greek island:

Day 1: Arrival and Relaxation

- **Afternoon:** Arrive in Skiathos and check into your accommodation. Choose a hotel or villa with a private balcony or pool for ultimate privacy.
- **Evening:** Enjoy a leisurely stroll through Skiathos Town, exploring the narrow, whitewashed streets, charming boutiques, and picturesque harbor. Indulge in a romantic dinner at a waterfront taverna, savoring fresh seafood and local wine while watching the sunset.

Day 2: Beach Hopping and Adventure

- **Morning:** Rent a scooter or ATV for a fun and adventurous way to explore the island. Head to the secluded beach of Lalaria, famous for its crystal-clear waters and unique rock formations. Spend the day

swimming, sunbathing, and enjoying a picnic lunch.
- **Afternoon:** Return to Skiathos Town and take a leisurely boat trip to the nearby island of Skopelos, known for its lush greenery and picturesque villages. Explore the charming town of Skopelos and enjoy a delicious Greek lunch.
- **Evening:** Return to Skiathos and enjoy a romantic dinner at a secluded seaside restaurant.

Day 3: Island Exploration and Pampering

- **Morning:** Visit the Monastery of Evangelistria, a historic landmark with stunning views of the island. Take a guided tour to learn about the monastery's rich history and religious significance.
- **Afternoon:** Indulge in a couples' massage or spa treatment at a luxury hotel or spa. Relax and rejuvenate together, surrounded by tranquility.
- **Evening:** Enjoy a romantic dinner at a rooftop restaurant with panoramic views of the town and harbor.

Day 4: Sailing and Sunset Cruise

- **Afternoon:** Embark on a private sailing cruise around the island. Explore hidden coves, swim in crystal-clear waters, and enjoy a delicious lunch on board.
- **Evening:** Watch the sunset from the deck of your boat, with a glass of champagne in hand. Enjoy a romantic dinner on a secluded beach or at a beachfront taverna.

Day 5: Farewell to Paradise

- **Morning:** Enjoy a leisurely breakfast at your accommodation. Spend your last morning relaxing by the pool or exploring the local markets for souvenirs.
- **Afternoon:** Depart for the airport, cherishing the memories of your romantic escape to Skiathos.

Optional Activities:

- Visit the Papadiamantis House Museum, dedicated to the famous Greek writer.
- Take a cooking class to learn the secrets of Greek cuisine.
- Enjoy a romantic evening watching a movie under the stars at an outdoor cinema.

Remember, this is just a suggestion, and you can customize your itinerary based on your preferences and interests.Skiathos offers endless possibilities for romance, so let your hearts guide you!

12.3. Best Restaurants for Couples

Skiathos isn't just about sun-kissed beaches and vibrant nightlife; it's also a haven for romance. With its charming atmosphere and delectable cuisine, the island offers an array of enchanting restaurants perfect for couples seeking an intimate dining experience.

Fine Dining with a View

- **Infinity Blue:** Perched on a cliff with breathtaking panoramic views of the Aegean Sea, Infinity Blue offers an unforgettable culinary journey. Indulge in exquisite seafood dishes and savor the magic of a sunset dinner.
- **The Windmill:** A historic landmark transformed into a romantic restaurant, The Windmill boasts stunning views and a sophisticated ambiance. Enjoy a fusion of international and Greek cuisine while being captivated by the island's charm.

Intimate and Charming

- **Marmita:** Nestled in a traditional stone house with a beautiful garden, Marmita creates a magical atmosphere for couples. Savor the exquisite flavors of upscale Greek cuisine and let the enchanting surroundings set the mood.
- **Black Pepper:** Located within the Avalon Hotel, Black Pepper offers a refined dining experience with a poolside setting. The menu features a delightful blend of Mediterranean and Greek flavors, perfect for a romantic evening.

Seaside Serenity

- **Agnadio:** Enjoy a romantic dinner by the sea at Agnadio, where fresh seafood takes center stage. The restaurant's idyllic location and delicious cuisine create a truly unforgettable experience.
- **Exantas Bar Restaurant:** With its elegant ambiance and stunning sea views, Exantas is a perfect choice for couples seeking a sophisticated dining experience. Indulge in a variety of Mediterranean delicacies and let the gentle sea breeze add to the romance.

Remember: Reservations are highly recommended, especially during peak season, to ensure you secure a table at your desired restaurant.

Whether you prefer a sophisticated fine dining experience or a charming seaside taverna, Skiathos offers a diverse range of romantic restaurants to make your evening truly special.

12.4. Honeymoon Ideas

Skiathos is a dream destination for honeymooners seeking a blend of relaxation, romance, and adventure. With its pristine beaches, charming villages, and luxurious accommodations, the island sets the perfect stage for a truly unforgettable honeymoon.

Romantic Retreats:

- **Luxurious Villas:** Indulge in privacy and seclusion with a stunning villa boasting private pools, breathtaking views, and personalized services.
- **Boutique Hotels:** Experience the charm of boutique hotels offering intimate

atmospheres, personalized attention, and romantic amenities.
- **Beachfront Resorts:** Unwind in style at a beachfront resort with direct access to powdery sands and crystal-clear waters.

Intimate Experiences:

- **Sunset Cruises:** Sail into the sunset with your loved one, enjoying champagne and canapés as you watch the sky transform into a canvas of colors.
- **Private Beach Picnics:** Escape the crowds and enjoy a romantic picnic on a secluded beach, complete with gourmet delicacies and chilled champagne.
- **Spa Treatments:** Rejuvenate your senses with couples' massages or other pampering treatments at a luxurious spa.

Adventurous Spirits:

- **Island Hopping:** Explore the nearby islands of Skopelos and Alonissos, discovering hidden coves and charming villages together.
- **Water Sports:** Engage in thrilling water sports like jet skiing, paddleboarding, or snorkeling for an adrenaline rush.

- **Hiking:** Embark on romantic hikes through lush landscapes, enjoying breathtaking views and quality time together.

Culinary Delights:

- **Romantic Dinners:** Savor exquisite cuisine at a beachfront restaurant, candlelit tavern, or rooftop terrace with panoramic views.
- **Wine Tasting:** Discover the flavors of Greece with a wine tasting experience, learning about local varietals and pairing them with delicious cheeses and appetizers.
- **Cooking Classes:** Bond over shared culinary experiences by taking a cooking class together and learning to create authentic Greek dishes.

Unforgettable Moments:

- **Photography Sessions:** Capture the essence of your honeymoon with a professional photoshoot in stunning locations around the island.
- **Stargazing:** Spend a magical evening under the starry Greek sky, sharing dreams and making lifelong memories.

Whether you prefer relaxation, adventure, or a combination of both, Skiathos offers an idyllic setting for your honeymoon. Create unforgettable memories as you embark on this new chapter of your life together.

Chapter 13. Day Trips and Excursions

13.1. Nearby Islands

Skiathos is a fantastic base for exploring the enchanting Sporades archipelago. While the island itself boasts countless treasures, the surrounding islands offer unique experiences and breathtaking landscapes. Here's a glimpse of what awaits:

Skopelos: The Green Island

Just a short ferry ride away, Skopelos reveals its lush, emerald beauty. Known for its pine-clad hills, charming villages,and stunning beaches, Skopelos is a haven for nature lovers and those seeking a more relaxed pace.

- **Must-See:** The picturesque village of Glossa, with its winding cobblestone streets and panoramic views.
- **Beach Bliss:** Adorn yourself in a white dress and visit Agios Ioannis Kastri, the iconic church made famous by the movie *Mamma Mia*.

Alonissos: Marine Paradise

For a truly off-the-beaten-path adventure, head to Alonissos. This island is a gem for divers and snorkelers, boasting a protected marine park teeming with diverse marine life. Beyond the underwater wonders, Alonissos offers charming villages, secluded coves, and a laid-back atmosphere.

- **Underwater Exploration:** Discover the rich biodiversity of the Alonissos Marine Park.
- **Island Escape:** Relax on the pristine beaches of Patitiri or explore the traditional villages of Votsi and Steni Valia.

Skyros: Authentic Greece

Further afield but equally captivating is Skyros, the largest island in the Sporades. Known for its unique culture, traditions, and rugged landscapes, Skyros offers a glimpse into authentic Greece.

- **Cultural Immersion:** Experience the island's rich folklore and traditions.
- **Natural Beauty:** Hike through the mountains, explore hidden coves, or relax on secluded beaches.

Note: Ferry connections between the Sporades islands are frequent during the peak season, making island hopping a convenient and enjoyable experience.

Whether you're seeking vibrant nightlife, pristine beaches, or cultural immersion, the islands surrounding Skiathos offer something for every traveler. So, why not embark on a thrilling island-hopping adventure and discover the hidden gems of the Sporades?

13.2. Cultural and Historical Day Trips

While Skiathos boasts stunning beaches and vibrant nightlife, it's also a gateway to rich history and culture. Here are some captivating day trips to consider:

Island Hopping for History and Charm

- **Skopelos:** Known as the island where the iconic movie "Mamma Mia!" was filmed, Skopelos offers a blend of natural beauty and historical charm. Explore the picturesque port town, visit the charming villages of

Glossa and Panormos, and discover the island's rich Byzantine heritage.
- **Alonissos:** This serene island is a haven for nature lovers and history enthusiasts alike. Explore the charming port town of Patitiri, visit the historic monastery of Agios Dimitrios, and take a boat trip to the pristine Marine Park of Northern Sporades.

Mainland Adventures: Delve into Greece's Past

- **Volos:** This bustling port city offers a fascinating mix of history, culture, and modern life. Visit the Archaeological Museum to admire ancient artifacts, explore the charming Old Town, and savor delicious local cuisine.
- **Meteora:** A UNESCO World Heritage Site, Meteora is home to breathtaking monasteries perched on towering rock formations. Take a day trip to witness this awe-inspiring spectacle and learn about the rich monastic history of the region.

Sailing and Exploring: Discover Hidden Gems

- **Boat Excursions:** Embark on a boat trip to explore the hidden coves, beaches, and islets around Skiathos. Many tours include stops for swimming, snorkeling, and exploring historical sites like the Kastro, Skiathos' old capital.

Remember: When planning your day trips, consider your interests, time constraints, and preferred mode of transportation. Whether you're a history buff, a nature lover, or simply seeking a change of scenery, there's a perfect day trip waiting for you from Skiathos.

13.3. Nature and Adventure Day Trips

Skiathos isn't just about sun-kissed beaches and vibrant nightlife. The island offers a wealth of opportunities for nature lovers and adventure seekers. Here are some day trips to consider:

Island Hopping Adventures

- **Skopelos and Alonissos:** These neighboring islands offer a different pace from Skiathos. Skopelos is known for its lush greenery and charming villages, while

Alonissos is a haven for marine life. Boat trips often combine visits to both islands, allowing you to explore picturesque harbors, secluded beaches, and perhaps even spot dolphins in their natural habitat.

- **Day Sailing Cruise:** For a more intimate experience, consider a day sailing cruise around Skiathos. These trips often include stops for swimming and snorkeling in secluded coves, as well as opportunities to admire the coastline from a unique perspective.

Exploring the Island's Interior

- **Hiking and Trekking:** While Skiathos is primarily known for its beaches, the island also boasts some delightful hiking trails. Explore the island's interior, discover hidden coves, and enjoy panoramic views from the hilltops.
- **Kastro:** The old capital of Skiathos, Kastro, is a charming fortified town perched on a hilltop. Exploring its narrow, winding streets and admiring the stunning views is a must-do for history and culture enthusiasts.

Water-Based Adventures

- **Kayaking and Paddleboarding:** Explore the coastline at your own pace with kayaking or paddleboarding. Many companies offer guided tours or equipment rentals for independent adventurers.
- **Diving and Snorkeling:** Discover the underwater world with diving or snorkeling excursions. The crystal-clear waters around Skiathos are home to a vibrant marine ecosystem.

Day Trips with a Purpose

- **Boat Trip with a Cause:** Some boat trips offer a chance to contribute to conservation efforts. Visit marine sanctuaries, participate in clean-up initiatives, or support local wildlife conservation projects.

Remember to pack comfortable walking shoes, sunscreen, a hat, and plenty of water for your day trips. Whether you're seeking adventure, relaxation, or a combination of both, Skiathos has something to offer everyone.

Chapter 14. Events and Festivals

14.1. Annual Festivals

Skiathos isn't just about sun-kissed beaches and azure waters; it's also a vibrant island with a rich cultural heritage.Throughout the year, locals and visitors alike come together to celebrate with a series of captivating festivals. Here's a glimpse into some of the highlights:

Religious Celebrations

- **Agios Georgios (Saint George):** Celebrated on April 23rd (or the Monday after Easter if April 23rd falls during Holy Week), this festival is marked by horse races, delicious food, and the lively Kamara dance.
- **Panagia Evangelistria:** This monastery in the heart of the island hosts a feast on March 25th, offering a chance to explore its historical significance and soak in the serene atmosphere.
- **Dormition of the Virgin Mary:** On August 15th, the island comes alive with the largest summer festival, filled with religious ceremonies, traditional music, and dancing.

Commemorative Events

- **Katsonia Festival:** Held in September, this poignant festival honors the Greek submarine "Lambros Katsonis" that was tragically sunk off Skiathos during World War II. Locals pay tribute by casting flowers into the Aegean Sea.

Cultural Celebrations

- **Skiathos Fest:** This international folk dance and music festival brings together talented performers from around the world, creating a vibrant cultural exchange.
- **International Festival "Days in Skiathos":** Showcasing a diverse range of dance, music, and theater performances, this festival offers a captivating cultural experience.

Beyond these scheduled events, Skiathos often hosts spontaneous celebrations, such as local village festivals and open-air concerts. These impromptu gatherings provide an authentic taste of island life and a chance to mingle with friendly locals.

So, whether you're drawn to religious traditions, cultural performances, or simply the festive atmosphere, Skiathos offers a calendar brimming with events to enhance your island adventure.

Would you like to know about any specific festival in more detail?

14.2. Local Events Calendar

Skiathos isn't just about sun-kissed beaches and azure waters; it's also a vibrant island with a rich cultural heritage. Throughout the year, the island hosts a variety of events that offer visitors a glimpse into local traditions and festivities.

While specific dates and events may vary from year to year, here's a general overview of what you might encounter during your visit:

Summertime Celebrations

Summer is undoubtedly the peak season in Skiathos, and the island comes alive with a plethora of events:

- **Music Festivals:** Expect a vibrant music scene with live performances by both local and international artists. From traditional Greek music to contemporary beats, there's something for everyone.
- **Cultural Events:** Traditional dance performances, art exhibitions, and local craft

markets offer a taste of authentic Greek culture.
- **Village Festivals:** Many villages on the island host their own festivals, often featuring delicious local food, traditional music, and dancing.

Religious Festivities

Skiathos has a deep-rooted Orthodox Christian faith, and religious celebrations are an integral part of island life:

- **Name Days:** Greeks celebrate their name days with equal enthusiasm as birthdays. If you happen to share a name with a saint, you might be invited to join in the festivities.
- **Church Festivals:** Throughout the year, various churches on the island organize festivals (panigiria) in honor of their patron saints. These events typically involve religious ceremonies, traditional food, and dancing.

Other Notable Events

- **Skiathos Film Festival:** This annual event showcases both established and emerging

filmmakers, attracting film enthusiasts from around the world.
- **Sailing Regattas:** Skiathos is a popular destination for sailing enthusiasts, and several regattas take place throughout the summer.

Note: To get the most accurate and up-to-date information about events happening during your visit, check local listings, tourist information centers, or the official Skiathos website closer to your travel dates.

By immersing yourself in the local events, you'll gain a deeper appreciation for Skiathos' unique character and create unforgettable memories.

14.3. Celebrations and Traditions

Skiathos isn't just about sun-kissed beaches and azure waters. The island boasts a rich tapestry of traditions and festivals that offer a glimpse into the heart and soul of its people.

Religious Celebrations

Orthodox Christianity is deeply ingrained in Skiathos' culture, and religious festivals are a cornerstone of the island's calendar.

- **Easter:** A particularly poignant celebration, marked by somber rituals on Good Friday and culminating in joyous festivities on Easter Sunday.
- **Agios Georgios (St. George):** Celebrated on April 23rd (or the Monday after Easter), this festival honors the patron saint of shepherds and cavaliers with horse races and traditional dances.
- **Panagia Evangelistria:** The island's main monastery hosts a grand celebration on March 25th, attracting pilgrims from far and wide.

Local Festivals and Events

Beyond religious celebrations, Skiathos offers a vibrant calendar of events that showcase the island's unique character.

- **Katsonia Festival:** Held in September, this event commemorates the sinking of the Greek submarine "Lambros Katsonis" with a poignant floral tribute to the sea.

- **Bourtzi Festival:** This summer festival transforms the historic Bourtzi fortress into a cultural hub with theater performances, art exhibitions, concerts, and even traditional shadow puppetry.
- **Panigiri:** Throughout the year, villages across Skiathos host lively panigiri, traditional village festivals featuring delicious food, music, and dancing.

Traditions and Customs

Skiathos is steeped in customs that have been passed down through generations.

- **Hospitality:** The islanders are renowned for their warm welcome and generous hospitality, making visitors feel instantly at home.
- **Music and Dance:** Traditional Greek music and dance are an integral part of island life, often enjoyed at village squares and local taverns.
- **Cuisine:** Skiathos boasts a rich culinary heritage, with dishes like stuffed tomatoes, seafood delicacies, and honey-soaked pastries tempting taste buds.

Immerse yourself in the vibrant tapestry of Skiathos' celebrations and traditions to experience the island's authentic charm. Whether you're dancing under the stars, attending a religious ceremony, or simply enjoying a traditional meal, you'll create unforgettable memories.

Chapter 15. Practical Information

15.1. Emergency Contacts

While Skiathos is generally a safe island, it's always wise to be prepared. Here are essential emergency contact numbers to keep handy during your stay:

General Emergency Numbers:

- **European Emergency Number:** 112 (works for police, ambulance, and fire brigade)
- **Greek Police:** 100
- **Greek Ambulance:** 166
- **Greek Fire Brigade:** 199

Local Emergency Contacts:

- **Skiathos Health Center:** +30 24270 22222
- **Skiathos Police Station:** +30 24270 29152
- **Skiathos Port Authority:** +30 24270 22017

Additional Useful Numbers:

- **Tourist Police:** +30 24270 23172

- **Skiathos Airport:** +30 24270 22049

Important Note: It's recommended to save these numbers in your phone and have a physical copy as well.

Medical Emergencies:

While Skiathos has a health center, it's always advisable to have travel insurance that covers medical emergencies. It's also a good idea to pack a basic first-aid kit.

Remember: In case of an emergency, dial 112 immediately.

By being prepared with these essential contact numbers, you can enjoy your Skiathos vacation with added peace of mind.

15.2. Local Laws and Customs

While Skiathos is a welcoming and relaxed island, it's important to respect local laws and customs to ensure a smooth and enjoyable stay.

Laws and Regulations:

- **Respectful Attire:** While Greece is generally relaxed in terms of dress code, it's

advisable to dress modestly when visiting religious sites, such as monasteries.
- **Beach Behavior:** While enjoying the beautiful beaches, please respect other beachgoers by avoiding loud music and excessive noise.
- **Wildlife Protection:** Greece has strict laws protecting its wildlife and environment. Avoid disturbing or harming any animals or plants.
- **Photography:** It's generally acceptable to take photos, but it's polite to ask permission before photographing people, especially in private spaces.
- **Driving:** If you plan to rent a car, be aware that Greek driving can be different from what you're accustomed to. Drive defensively and obey traffic laws.

Local Customs and Etiquette:

- **Hospitality:** Greeks are known for their warm hospitality. A simple "kalimera" (good morning) or "kalispera" (good evening) goes a long way.
- **Pace of Life:** Embrace the relaxed island lifestyle. Things often happen at a slower pace, so be patient and enjoy the moment.

- **Mealtimes:** Lunch is typically served between 1-3 pm and dinner around 8-10 pm.
- **Tipping:** While tipping is not mandatory, it's customary to leave a small tip (around 10%) for good service at restaurants and bars.
- **Respect for Local Traditions:** Participate in local festivals and events with an open mind and respect for local customs.

By understanding and respecting these local laws and customs, you'll contribute to a positive and enjoyable experience for yourself and the locals.

15.3. Internet and Connectivity

While disconnecting from the world can be part of the charm of a Greek island getaway, it's good to know your options when it comes to staying connected in Skiathos.

Mobile Data and Wi-Fi

- **Mobile Data:** Most major international carriers offer roaming services in Greece. However, data roaming can be expensive. It's advisable to check with your provider before your trip. Alternatively, you can purchase a

local SIM card upon arrival for more affordable data options.
- **Wi-Fi:** Many hotels, restaurants, and cafes in Skiathos offer free Wi-Fi. The quality and speed can vary, but it's generally sufficient for basic browsing and social media. Additionally, the island has free public Wi-Fi hotspots in certain areas, thanks to the WiFi4EU initiative.

Internet Cafes

While less common than in the past, there are still a few internet cafes in Skiathos Town if you need a reliable connection for tasks requiring high-speed internet.

Important Note: Signal strength can vary depending on your location, especially in remote areas. It's always a good idea to have a backup plan, such as downloading offline maps or essential information before your trip.

By understanding your connectivity options, you can balance staying connected with enjoying the island's laid-back atmosphere.

Chapter 16. Useful Resources

16.1. Travel Apps and Websites

Navigating a new destination can be made much easier with the right digital tools. Here are some apps and websites that can enhance your Skiathos experience:

Essential Travel Apps:

- **Google Maps:** A must-have for exploring the island, finding points of interest, and navigating public transportation.
- **Booking.com or Airbnb:** For finding accommodations that suit your preferences and budget.
- **TripAdvisor:** Read reviews, discover attractions, and find restaurants.
- **WhatsApp:** A reliable messaging app for staying connected with friends, family, and local contacts.
- **Currency Converter:** Convert Euros to your home currency on the fly.
- **Translation App:** Useful for basic communication with locals who don't speak English.

Helpful Websites:

- **Visit Skiathos:** The official tourism website offers comprehensive information about the island, including attractions, events, and accommodation options.
- **Ferry Booking Websites:** If you plan on island hopping, websites like Ferryhopper or Hellenic Seaways can help you book ferry tickets.
- **Weather Apps:** Check the weather forecast before planning your daily activities.

Additional Tips:

- **Offline Maps:** Download offline maps for Google Maps or use dedicated offline map apps to save data and navigate without an internet connection.
- **Free Wi-Fi:** Many cafes, restaurants, and hotels offer free Wi-Fi. However, having a local SIM card with data can be convenient for staying connected on the go.
- **App Store Research:** Explore the app store for specific apps related to your interests, such as food, beach activities, or water sports.

By utilizing these digital tools, you can make the most of your time in Skiathos and ensure a smooth and enjoyable trip.

16.2. Contact Information for Tourist Services

While Skiathos doesn't have a dedicated tourist information office, there are several resources available to assist visitors:

Local Tourist Information:

- **I Love Skiathos:** This website and social media channels offer comprehensive information about the island, including accommodation, activities, and events. They can also be contacted directly for inquiries.
    - Website: http://www.iloveskiathos.gr/
    - Email: skiathosapp@gmail.com
    - Phone: +30 695 577 7454
- **G.A.T.S. Travel Skiathos:** This travel agency offers a range of services including tours, accommodation, and transportation. They can provide tourist information and assistance.
    - Website: http://www.gatstravel.gr/
    - Phone: +30 2427 024226

Other Helpful Resources:

- **Tourist Police:** While not a dedicated information center, the tourist police can provide assistance and information to visitors.
    - Phone: +30 24270 23172
- **Local Businesses:** Hotels, restaurants, and shops often have staff who can offer recommendations and information about the island.

Note: While these resources can provide valuable information, it's always a good idea to do your own research before your trip and have a general understanding of what you want to see and do in Skiathos.

By utilizing these contact points and conducting your own research, you can make the most of your time on this beautiful island.

Chapter 17. Conclusion

17.1. Final Tips and Advice

Skiathos is ready to enchant you with its beauty and charm. To make the most of your trip, consider these final tips:

- **Embrace the Island Pace:** While Skiathos offers plenty to do, remember to relax and soak up the island's laid-back atmosphere.
- **Explore Beyond the Main Town:** Venture beyond Skiathos Town to discover hidden coves, charming villages, and authentic experiences.
- **Indulge in Local Cuisine:** Savor the fresh seafood, delicious mezedes, and local wines that Skiathos has to offer.
- **Respect the Environment:** Help preserve Skiathos' natural beauty by respecting the environment and supporting eco-friendly businesses.
- **Learn a Few Greek Phrases:** A little effort goes a long way in connecting with the locals and enriching your experience.
- **Capture the Moments:** Don't forget to capture the stunning landscapes, vibrant sunsets, and unforgettable memories.

With its pristine beaches, rich history, and warm hospitality, Skiathos promises an unforgettable vacation. Enjoy your time on this enchanting island!

The Nymph of Skiathos

In the beginning, when the world was young, and the gods walked the earth, there was an island born of froth and sunlight. It was Skiathos, a jewel in the Aegean Sea. And on this island lived a nymph, named Thalassa, as beautiful as the sea that cradled her home.

Thalassa was the spirit of the island, her laughter the gentle lapping of waves, her tears the rain that nourished the land. She danced with the dolphins, rode the backs of sea turtles, and sang to the rhythm of the wind. The gods fell in love with her spirit, and mortals were drawn to her beauty.

One summer, a mortal prince, sailing the seas, was captivated by the island's allure. Drawn to its shores, he met Thalassa. Their love was a tempest, as passionate as the sea, as pure as the sky. The prince vowed to protect her island forever.

But the gods, jealous of their mortal's happiness, sent a great storm to test the prince's love. The waves crashed against the shore, threatening to swallow the island. The prince, with a heart filled with courage, stood firm, his arms outstretched as if to shield Thalassa.

When the storm passed, the island was untouched, a testament to the prince's love. But Thalassa, weary from the ordeal, transformed herself into the island's lush greenery, her spirit forever intertwined with its soul. And so, it is said, that the essence of Thalassa lives on in Skiathos, in the whisper of the pines, the kiss of the sun, and the magic that captivates all who visit her shores.

And that is why Skiathos holds such a special place in the hearts of those who discover her. It is an island blessed by the gods, a haven of peace and beauty, where the spirit of a nymph still resides.

Printed in Great Britain
by Amazon